"This book explains structure your own ch communicating with c become a great leader."

Pungky Sumadi - Deputy Minister for Population and Employment ,The National Development Planning Agency (BAPPENAS) of the Republic of Indonesia.

"Cultural intelligence (ICQ) has been essential to level up my self-awareness, self-esteem, and personal growth. Is now the foundation of my coaching practice and how I create an impact on individuals and organisations. The insights that "Uncommon sense in unusual times" brings to the table are essential to study and practice for anyone who aims to engage and lead in this Global world and during this unusual and VUCA times."

Sinto Llobera - CEO of ICQ Global Asia

"Uncommonly sensible, that's how I describe Csaba Toth's successful expedition to join two significant strands of 20th century theory into a 21st century framework to solve the perils of globalisation. If we don't get inclusion right in the next 10 years, we're destined for less creative, less fair and less fun workplaces. For people working and consulting in diverse workplaces, you have to have a cultural perspective. You need a global mindset. Humanity may have access to more advanced and instantaneous translation than ever before, but even when we speak the same language, we can experience great gaps in understanding. Gaps that lead to confusion, conflict and disengagement. Tools that help you step out of cultural, personal and professional biases and into creative forms of communication and collaborative action are essential. Csaba's book can help you overcome the perils and realize the potential of globalisation. I know, I have been using the tools successfully for a number of years in my own

business and my clients are the ones reaping the benefits of a simple and yet powerful tool to make sense of our unusual times. Drop MBTI, Insights, and DISC. Go Global DISC."

Skip Bowman, CEO and Founder,
Global Mindset, Copenhagen

"The book takes me step by step and immerses me to the knowledge of what is culture, why people behave so differently, why so many times people just accept the way they do things in a certain way. It is comprehensive and easy to understand. It includes many examples and illustrations in the day to day the way the business is run. The book provides effective methods and techniques for leaders."

Retno Nartani - Director HSE Corporate
PT. Golden Energy Mines, Sinarmas
Mining Group

"This is the book I've been waiting for! Not only does it give a brilliant introduction to the science of intercultural intelligence, but also gives the keys for getting along with people who are different to ourselves."

Satya Tanner - Leadership and VUCA
Skills Coach www.satyatanner.com

"Change, intercultural, coaching, self-awareness, and innovation are some of the most leading notions in my everyday professional life, and I am delighted to have found them all together. The book put forward a paradigm shift combining personality types and cultural dimensions, traditional notions are revisited, intercultural finds its way not limited to country specificities, gender or generations, and coaching is invited to the game. Self-awareness is offered from two perspectives : the author's experience, learning and vulnerability and an interactive online Quest for the reader to explore the topics *addressed in the book. A XXI Century approach to move forward in better living together!"*

Jimena Andino Dorato - Certified
Coach & Money Coach

"Csaba's book is an authentic, eye opening and a thought provoking one about cultural intelligence, based on his own experiences. It helped me in identify my own life and career goals as well as upgrade my personal and business relationships. I suggest you read it, reflect on it and experience the Quest, so it can be life and career changing for you, too."

Janos Laincsek - CEO of ICQ Global Hungary

"I first met Csaba in March 2013 when I was looking to connect with intercultural facilitators on a trip to Europe. He generously shared with me an early iteration of Global DISC in its infancy. Some six years later it is with great pleasure and vicarious pride that I am able to share in the launch of Csaba's book, "Uncommon Sense in Unusual Times." It is a well-written quick moving, practical and informative insight into how to learn, sharpen and polish Cultural Intelligence as the essential 21st century leadership skill. For me, Csaba brings this lifelong quest back to the human level and where we began as people, "How do we connect and move forward together to achieve a common goal?"

Holona Lui - Director, Catalyst Pacific
Ltd, Aotearoa, New Zealand

"This book, "Uncommon sense" is an excellent eye-opener for Leaders and all Others who are faced with the daily challenges of working and living in our increasingly complex global Environment. It addresses the whole spectrum of change in a global and culturally diverse Environment by focusing on the "why, how and what" of all challenges and misconceptions we

need to constructively deal with in this increasingly complex global environment. Applying ICQ is according to my professional experience as an HR leader and my life as a "global citizen" a condicio sine qua non " to learn to master our complex mind to ensure we evolve from a survival to creation state of being. "

Gwen Murray - co-founder and managing partner of "People Change Synapse"

"This book has a fresh and uncomplicated approach on cultural intelligence, global mindset, leadership and our relationship with people. The content is rooted in Csaba's research and belief that intercultural is not just international but interpersonal. Each chapter is rich with references, his experiences and things that most of us experience. This book is not an empty show of virtuosity because at the end of the book each reader will get a free Global DISC assessment, a blueprint of their own mindset and an interactive coaching platform to put theory into practice."

Wieke Gur - CEO of ICQ Global Indonesia, Global DISC Master Trainer

"Csaba's book is excellent and profound in many ways. It invites us to deep-level reflection on diversity and inclusion and provides hands-on solutions for dealing with complex situations. In an accessible and easy to understand way he explains the importance of self-inclusion and the ability to decode cognitive diversity for creating an inclusive environment. Combining the neuroscientific principles with latest business research Csaba's book will help you boost your Cultural Intelligence for high performance in challenging environments."

Anna Zelno - Shortlisted for European Diversity Awards as Inspirational Role Model 2019, Intercultural Trainer and Diversity Management Consultant

"The arrival of 'Uncommon Sense in Unusual Times' could not be timelier: Globalisation presents us with tremendous VUCA challenges that can no longer be resolved single-handedly. Yet, more and more nations, businesses and individuals are turning their back on connecting and collaborating with other cultures. Only when we are able to bridge distances between people, practice tolerance, and solve conflicts by joining together through ICQ-Cultural Intelligence can we find sustainable solutions for our future to thrive. Csaba in his book does not only offer a well-researched comprehensive and long-overdue definition of culture and busts all the misperceptions that come with it; and with Global DISC™ he also provides THE cutting-edge approach to ICQ-Cultural Intelligence. It is a self-awareness and communication tool that no interculturalist, global leader, nor business can do without anymore, if they want to be able to understand and leverage personal and cultural differences to successfully serve their customers, teams, partners, colleagues in the best possible way: professionally, effectively and with integrity. Highly practical and recommendable!"

Marina Ibrahim - AWARD-WINNING Global &
Cultural Agility Coaching & Training
Consultant, www.globility-coaching.com

"Sensing capability is critical for leaders in the world of connectivity. Many knows where to go, or at least putting serious effort to define the finish line – sadly, few really spend time to understand where to start. No wonder we see lots of frustration from leaders desperately wanting to make changes. And one thing that get the most complained is "behaviour". Most of us understand there are many drivers for behaviour. Yet, we still ignoring that fact when we have to deal with specific behaviour. This book will challenge our habit in approaching people issue and it will provide us with a simple structure to understand the why, what, and how of day-to-day behaviour we see. Good

ingredients for leaders willing to harness their sensing capability and to be more effective in day-to-day job."

Hendro Fujiono ST., MS., PhD. - Practical
Change Management Expert/Coach,
FujiShepherd & Associates

"Csaba's writing style is unique; his ideas are unconventional; his book is conversational, jargon-free and witty. The content is persuasive, practical and theoretically underpinned at the same time. If you are a change maker, or a manager at any level or a person working within cross-functional teams in your organization, this book is for you. Do you care deeply about diversity and inclusion? Do you fancy creating connected global teams in a disconnected world – a world where conflicts, differences of opinions and perspectives, aggressions and microaggressions affect the mental health of workplaces? Whenever decision-making becomes risky in fast-paced businesses, we hesitate to accept that "our almost perfect view of the world" might be flawed with cognitive biases and cultural filters. If you wish to go beyond your biases, achieve cognitive and situational flexibility in your work, this book will definitely offer you the insights and the necessary mind-set maintenance to excel in a world craving for authenticity and connection."

Mithun Mridha - PPM Practice Manager and
Enterprise Architect, Altran

"Every Leader & want to be Leader will find this book an essential read to develop their skill set and self awareness. The author has pulled diverse threads together with an ease of understanding & interesting reading allowing us to realise the impact we have on our results and others across cultural differences."

Julie Hogbin - Author & Conscious Leadership
& Skillful Speech Strategist, CLAVEM.global

"I have had the unique privilege of knowing and discussing Csaba's thinking on Leadership fit for the 21st Century over the past 3 years. This book is a combination of his work so far and further explains the genius behind his thinking on organisational thinking and leadership. As we launch into the New Decade I would recommend that Every CEO , Entrepreneur and Business Owner Reads this book not once but several times. This book should be a must read for everyone Leadership and Executive Coach on the planet. Its thought provoking and insightful on every single page."

Jim Jordan - Business Mentor and Executive Coach, www.jimjordanconsultancy.com

"Uncommon Sense in Unusual Times is an amazing and complete trip through the state of the art in management. We are in the 21st century, and we have just started a new decade. Management theories and skills are passing by an important evolution: how important is the diversity, inclusion, the correct use of mindsets, bias, the development of intercultural and interpersonal skills is finally been discussed and applied. However, all these concepts are still being considered isolated, incompletely, or superficially. But not in Uncommon Sense in Unusual Times. In this book we can better understand each one of these concepts, deeply, and to see how they are connected. As result, we really feel ourselves with consistent tools to deal with management, from the knowledge and management of our own lives, until the management in huge and complex organizations worldwide."

Renata Bohomoletz - Intercultural Strategic Management

"The world is complicated and we need a plan and a map to make sense of it. In a world that is both growing and shrinking, getting more diverse yet more polarised, more global yet more inward facing, Csaba's book is both the map and the plan we have been waiting for. Our innate 'common sense' – learnt from our own experiences – simply does not equip us to cope with the unexpected, but this 'guidebook' and quest does. By showing us not just what gaps we might fall into, but why, he helps us to understand better why those gaps have dogged us in the past and how we can learn how to navigate and even avoid them using 'un-common sense'. It is a life-skill we all need to acquire and this book is a great place to start."

Patti McCarthy - author Cultural Chemistry:
Simple Strategies for Bridging Cultural Gaps

"Brace yourself for Csaba Toth's book on Uncommon Sense! Like the title suggests, he will challenge many of your basic assumptions on how people think, bond, fail and succeed. The journey proposed here is fast and eventful, and completing it requires an open mind. But those who read this volume, whether they agree or disagree with its contents, will see human personality, communities and cultures in a different light."

Gábor Holch - Shanghai-based intercultural
management consultant, author and speaker

"The problem with traditional cross-cultural studies is that it ignores individual behaviours and the problem with individual behavioural profiling is that it ignores cultures. Csaba has been able to combine these two areas of study to create new models that are desperately needed for 21st century global leadership. Uncommon Sense should be on any global executive's reading list."

Kyle D. Hegarty - author of The Accidental
Business Nomad: A Survival Guide for
Working Across a Shrinking Planet

"A highly detailed, resource-rich book for intelligent global leaders and coaches to leverage the cognitive diversity and uncommon sense of their teams for success in the complex business world of today and tomorrow."

David Clive Price - Global Leadership & High Performance Coach, Author of Bamboo Strong

"As a training and coaching company in Central-Eastern Europe we've faced several business challenges with our clients from very different countries in the last 25 years. One of the key topics is positive mentality. We truly believe that high quality connections and high performing teams are the key in a VUCA world. Csaba's work and the Global DISC model is a fundamental, complex and inspiring help for our trainings, workshops and coaching sessions."

Szalay Zsuzsanna – CEO of Profil Training, www.profiltraining.hu

"In a world of global dynamics and urgently needed insightful leadership at all levels, Uncommon Sense in Unusual Times is an essential read, highlighting the dynamic interconnection between personality and culture. Csaba Toth compellingly makes the point that cultural intelligence is about more than country specific differences and introduces the practical GLOBAL DISC model as a valuable tool for everyone to act with wisdom, personally and professionally."

Birgit Trauer – author of The Way of the Peaceful Traveller

"In times such as this, adaptability is called for, less you wanted to extinct. This book forces us to have a deeper introspection on who we are. It gives us deeper insights in understanding how our relationships with others and the environment around us impact our mindset as individuals and those whom we are connected with as a whole.

Csaba's honest and raw revelation of his own experiences and studies made me rethink of my own perspective about culture. In fact, he has inspired me to modify my approach in teaching. I've integrated his research and concepts from this book and utilized Global DISC assessment and Quest in my class. Let me share two of my students' feedback after the integration:

"...The (cultural) class was an academic bridge between the (Global DISC) test/Quest and our true selves." - French student

" I wish we have had this class during middle school or even high school. I feel like I have missed out on many opportunities only because I was not aware of the influence culture has on people... and the reason I act in a certain way in certain situations. This class, followed by the Quest, made me dig deeper... Seeing them (others) being proud of some characteristics and struggling with the rest makes sense..." - Iranian student

Thank you Csaba for this practical and enriching book! It's a must read for every Cultural Trainers and Teachers!"

Cecilia Mag-isa Estoque - Filipino Professor
in one of China's State University

"Up to date, relevant and fluid, Csaba's book about Uncommon Sense is a fantastic piece to read for anybody looking into improving their interpersonal skills. With the right balance of theory, science and practical experience, you will not only grow while reading, you will also understand how - and why - you could impact and make the best out of your interactions in life. As a cross cultural leader for a global organisation in the field of HR, *not only am I confronted to this major challenge on a daily basis, I am the witness of global team leaders countless headache to addressing such complex field of management... From the moment I started to leverage my cross cultural intelligence skills (ICQ), thanks to the Global DISC, I got aware and confident in my abilities to embrace change in myself, and without even forcing it, in others. Be an ICQpreneur, be different, be you!"*

Stéphane Jaime Orts - International Business Manager @Catenon & Founder @Haute Culture

"This is not only a book for business owners at every level, but humans in general. The concepts of diversity and culture do not exist solely in a corporate vacuum, we are culture, we are diversity. Csaba cuts right to chase in identifying our flawed understanding of these topics and equips you with research and science-backed clarity while also providing a clear process and system for shifting our mindset and taking the action needed to facilitate the progress and synergy we all desire."

Tanya MFK - Business Strategy Consultant & Host of My Designed Life Show

"An extraordinarily valuable book for those who are interested in efficiency and effectiveness in the new era of leveraging relationships! As many of us want to get things done these days, and this requires an understanding of what makes us more or less make sense as we engage with our world and the critical people in it, this book should be considered a prime resource!

This book is a remarkable collection of proven developmental strategies and prospectives. Clear and fascinating, it is a must-read for those who aim to sharpen their interpersonal effectiveness.

I was stunned by ICQ and its ability to hit so many aspects of current cultural challenges and opportunities. ICQ delivers instant validation and inspired interpretations of many global and international relationship challenges."

Sameeh Gadallah - Intercultural business Coach/Consultant to help leaders connecting dots in the Middle East and Gulf region.

Uncommon Sense in Unusual Times

Csaba Toth

Uncommon Sense in Unusual Times

Published by Authorsunite.com

Dedicated to:

- The unnecessarily ruined relationships due to clashes of common senses and to the ones that survived and thrived
- All the growth-minded and courageous partners who challenge the status quo for the right reasons and spread the science of uncommon sense in all its shapes and forms

Table of Contents

Preface

Uncommon Sense in Unusual Times is based on 15 years of professional and personal failures and successes. Although nowadays it's trendy to encourage people to fail fast so they can learn quickly, I urge you instead to learn from other people's mistakes and achievements. It can save you years of frustration and pain.

When I moved to the UK from Hungary, I came to realise cultural differences exist as much between countries as within them. If we clash with someone in our own country, we call it 'personal differences.' When we have the same issues with someone of a different nationality, we often dismiss them as 'cultural differences'. In reality, they are one and the same, and both provide opportunities for growth.

How many times have you felt someone you were talking to had no common sense at all? That they just did not 'get' you? Chances are they had the same feeling about you, though maybe for a different reason. **Cultural differences (including so-called personal differences) are primarily clashes of common senses**. They do not have to lead to an intellectual or emotional battle with a binary win-lose outcome as **we are equally different and uniquely normal in our own way**.

I have spent most of my professional life trying to crack the code of why people think and behave differently, so we can get along personally and get ahead professionally. During that time, I have had the privilege to work with leading experts in the fields of coaching, leadership, and intercultural management. I have also trained hundreds of leaders, coaches, and entrepreneurs around the world. We have learned a lot from one another every single time.

Uncommon Sense in Unusual Times is based on those conversations, lessons, and research. It is for people whose success depends on how much they understand themselves and others. If you read the book as a standalone, it will enable you to understand seemingly common-sense concepts from different angles, so you can make better decisions.

The next step is to be able to respond instead of just reacting, and this is where the Uncommon Sense Quest interactive coaching platform can help you. This ICQ Global program will push you out of your comfort zone a little more every time you engage with it. Each mission in your Quest is based on a chapter in the book. You can read a chapter, reflect on it, and start your Quest. You can choose to do the work simultaneously by reading a chapter and then completing a mission. Or you can finish the book first and then begin your Quest.

This is not a tricky attempt on my part to upsell anything. Email me the receipt of your book at uncommonsense@ICQ. global, with **ICQpreneur** in the subject line, and I will send you a coupon to give you 100% discount.

The course also includes a free Global DISC assessment for you (usually priced at £97) and a ICQ Growth Mindset Certificate (usually priced at £290) as a well-deserved gift when you finish.

What you learn in this book might go against what you thought you believed to be true. My goal is not to convince you otherwise but to create a conversation, share insights, and come up with even better solutions.

PART ONE

Mindset Reboot

The Platinum Rule®
by Dr Tony Alessandra

An indisputable business fact is that people do business with people they like. It makes sense, therefore, to like and be liked by as many people as possible. The ability to create rapport with a large number of people is a fundamental skill in sales, management, personal relationships, and everyday life.

However, most of us never figure people out. We get along great with some people, refuse to deal with others, or deal as little as possible with still others, because they are so different from us.

But, what if you knew the secret of those differences? What if there was a simple, but proven, way to build rapport with everyone? To eliminate personality conflicts? To take charge of your own compatibility? To make business mutually beneficial instead of a contest of wills?

You literally hold such a key in your hands. A product of psychological research and practical application, the Platinum Rule® is a proven method of connecting with anyone in the workplace.

You can learn to handle people the way they want to be handled ... to speak to them in the way they are comfortable listening ... to sell to people the way they like to buy ... to lead people in ways that are comfortable for them to follow.

In business, especially, people all too often create tension and discomfort by assuming we are all pretty much alike. In fact, most of us, if asked about a philosophy of personal relations, probably would recall the Golden Rule that we learned as kids: "Do unto others as you would have them do unto you."

The downside of the Golden Rule

That is an old and honorable sentiment. Much good has been done in the world by people practicing the Golden Rule. As a guide to personal values, it can be a powerful force for honesty and compassion. However, as a yardstick for interpersonal communication, the Golden Rule has a downside.

If applied verbatim, it can actually cause personality conflicts. Why? Because literally following the Golden Rule—treating people the way **you** would like to be treated—means dealing with others from your own perspective, which can mean turning off those who have different needs, desires, and hopes than us.

Instead, I suggest honoring the real intent of the Golden Rule by modifying that ancient axiom just a bit. I think the secret to better relationships is to apply what I call the Platinum Rule®: "Do unto others as they'd like done unto them."

That means learning to really understand other people and then handling them in a way that is best for them, not just for us. It means taking the time to figure out the people around us and adjusting our behavior to make them more comfortable. It means using our knowledge and our tact to try to put others at ease. That, I suggest, is the true spirit of the Golden Rule. So the Platinum Rule® is not at odds with the Golden Rule. Instead, you might say, it is a newer, more sensitive version.

Not manipulation

Another important point: When I talk about using the Platinum Rule®, I am *not* talking about manipulating people! But, rather, learning, in a way, to speak their language.

4

It is not, for example, considered manipulative to speak French when in Paris. *Au contraire!* It is something you do briefly while on the Frenchman's soil so you can be more compatible. You do not alter your basic nature while in France. Your ideas do not change. However, *how* you present those ideas does change.

Similarly, practicing the Platinum Rule® does not fundamentally change you or the other person. It empowers you by making you, in a sense, multilingual. Knowing how to listen and speak in the "language" of those around you is a delightful, useful tool that can be used to resolve differences, maximize strengths, and enjoy a fuller, more successful life by better understanding yourself and the people around you.

The Platinum Rule® *model spans all cultures BUT it is important to remember that people around the world are socialised* into a certain preferred way of behaving and the Global DISC model explains why. It is a practical framework based on the most researched cross-cultural models to explain how national, cultural values and beliefs shape our behaviour.

This is the ideal tool in today's fast-paced, globalised world where the new generation of businesspeople and leaders need to be culturally intelligent and adaptable without being experts in hundreds of different cultures. Global DISC takes the Platinum Rule® *into deeper layers of understanding people so they can be treated the way they want and need to be treated. The more you understand people, the better rapport you will have with them,* which ultimately guarantees better interpersonal results.

CHAPTER **1**

Why Is Uncommon Sense So Important?

We often use words and phrases we never really define for ourselves. *Common sense* is one of those. According to the dictionary, common sense means "good sense and sound judgment in practical matters" or "sound judgment derived from experience rather than study". There are a few challenges with the concept:

- **Common sense is subjective.** It's based on our personal experience, not facts. If we don't have any actual experience, then we rely on the not overly reliable but steady stream of information sourced from social media, TV, and friends, or we make assumptions.
- **Common sense is not an exact science.** Most groups develop a set of unwritten rules to help their members navigate complex social interactions and ensure the smooth running of the community. Those rules make life more predictable, certain, and familiar. After all, that is what we like and trust.

- **Common sense is not a common practice.** Knowing something is not the same as doing it. I'm sure most of us have experienced that applying common sense can be difficult. For instance, changing habits is tricky. We know what's in our best interest, but being on autopilot, or feeling tired, stressed, or hungry, can hijack our best intentions, and we revert to a primal state of instant gratification.

It is common sense the sun rises in the east and sets in the west. The fact is, the sun doesn't do either. Because the earth rotates around the sun, sunrise and sunset are only perception. It is also common sense that basketball players are tall so it would make sense to play basketball if we wanted to be taller?

What's more, sometimes even the smallest discrepancies between what we think we know and what we see can throw us off. When I tried a new stevia-based coke in the USA this year, I couldn't make sense of it at all. It looked like lemonade, but it tasted like Pepsi. The experience was surreal, a tiny but disturbing instance of cognitive dissonance, the mental discomfort triggered when belief clashes with new evidence. As Warren Buffet said: "What the human being is best at doing is interpreting all new information so that their prior conclusions remain intact."

When something doesn't make sense to us, we react with surprise or annoyance, depending on the meaning we attach to the situation.

Let me give you an example. One of my first jobs in the UK was in a hotel, and it was a lot of fun. One day I was talking to one of the managers, who was also a friend of mine, and he said, "You Commies are not supposed to smile." Out of context, his comment could easily be perceived as offensive, borderline racist, a case any No Win No Fee solicitor would be happy to take on, but in this case we both understood it was really a compliment. Still, it was an interesting example of the sort of remark that can trigger strong assumptions and stereotypes. It all depends on the intention of the person making the comment and the interpretation of the person hearing it.

Cultural intelligence, or **ICQ,** introduces us to a wide range of approaches to common sense—and intention, context, and interpretation—and gives us strategies not only to help us tolerate them but to make the most of our differences. My goal in this book is to make this process as uncomplicated and practical as possible, to empower people to unlock their own potential, and to inspire others to create synergy with them.

But first I have to acknowledge common sense and good intention can dramatically backfire. This is where understanding the science of uncommon sense can be crucial. My story is a prime example of that.

From Hungarian boy to British lord

I grew up in a small town in Hungary where I had no contact with different cultures, or at least that's what I assumed at the time. *Culture* is a fancy word we use, often without thinking about its actual meaning. Growing up, I associated culture with the kind of activities I found boring: going to the theatre with my class, visiting a museum I wasn't interested in, or listening to classical music that annoyed me. Like most teenagers, I would have preferred watching a good movie instead.

Later on, I took culture to mean different nationalities; they were pretty much synonyms in my mind. And while not completely incorrect, it's most certainly incomplete. Today I understand I was surrounded by and belonged to several cultural groups, although I did not know it at the time. What I definitely knew was interacting with other people, or even with ourselves, can sometimes be difficult, frustrating, pleasant, fun, and infuriating all at once. It can make us feel alive or it can drive us mad.

Even back then, I was fascinated by the human mind. I really wanted to understand why people were so different, why we feel some lack common sense, why we might hit it off immediately with someone from the other side of the globe but clash with people we grew up with. I figured there must be logic in it, but as it wasn't real science in my parents' eyes, I had to study something useful.

Well, that was the plan.

Awakening the geek within

As I had no idea what I wanted to do in life, I got a master's degree in Italian linguistics and put all my energy into researching a 'life-changing' topic, proverbs. Or, to be more precise, my dissertation was about Italian, English, and Hungarian proverbs containing the words *dog* and *horse*. You might think it wasn't the most useful niche to pick (and I would agree with you), but that is where I found my passion. I just did not realise it back then.

Proverbs are a condensed knowledge and experience of previous generations, and they can offer much wisdom if we are willing to pay attention. Let's be honest, modern science often just confirms and explains what people have known for thousands of years. Our ancestors may not have known why something worked, but they certainly knew when it did, and they wanted to share this knowledge. Proverbs are smart, pithy messages that pass on advice from our forebears to help us avoid repeating their mistakes. That is how culture slowly evolves.

What I found fascinating—on top of the advice hidden in those primal twitter updates—was how proverbs reflect the cultural background and heritage of their group. For instance, if you work very hard, then in Hungarian you work like a horse, in Italian you work like an ox, and in English you work like a slave. Same concept, similar message, different expression.

My research was so successful it was published in a book in Italy as a PhD study. In fact, I never started my PhD program but came to the UK for a summer as soon as I graduated. Again, that was just a plan, and I have been here for 15 years.

10

Low-budget fairy tale

Weird story, but here it is in a nutshell. When I was about ten years old, I started collecting the new 20–forint coins. They were gold coloured, big, and the highest denomination I could take from my parents' wallets without getting into trouble. The coins were worth around 3–4 pence (£0.03), but they made me feel rich, so I put them in a metal box, and when it was full, I sealed and hid it. Twelve years later, I exchanged them all and got around £300, which covered an open return coach ticket to the UK and two days in a hostel. I had no job, no accommodation, and finding both in Brighton in the summer, especially without money or connections, was pretty impossible. At the end of my second day, I found myself packing my bag again. My plan was to go back to Victoria Station in London and stay there until I could head home. I was almost ready to leave when two Polish girls knocked on the door, urgently looking for housemates as they had found a cheap house to rent for the summer. What were the chances!

This beginning was quite typical for somebody from a newly joined EU country with a few non-transferrable skills and no real-life experience. I cleaned hotel rooms until they were sparkling again and then worked my way into the hospitality industry, running events for up to 600 people and managing restaurants. In the meantime, I never stopped learning and saving up money, which allowed me to get another master's degree from the University of Sussex. The Science Policy Research Unit (SPRU) was number two in the world in terms of research impact on innovation studies and number one in development studies.

But here I experienced some confusion again. Despite the fact it was a world-class institution, the work seemed much easier than in Hungary. There I had to study for five years, take a lot of exams, give presentations, and at the end defend my dissertation. The Sussex course took me nine months, during which I attended class once a week and had three jobs on the side. How could it be the best?

Then I realised they were two completely different approaches. In Hungary, my studies focused on facts and lexical knowledge. I was considered smart if I could memorise 80% of the book. Here in the UK I was considered smart if I could think and challenge the status quo. Back in Hungary you didn't do that unless you intentionally decided to fail or leave the university. Hopefully the situation has changed since then.

The competitive advantage I had was the work ethic I acquired studying for my first degree, which I combined with the new approach at Sussex. One was not better than the other. Both had advantages and disadvantages, and all I had to do was to pick and choose what served me best.

My dissertation was more practical this time: "The implications of organisational learning in Eastern and Western European joint ventures".

I replicated a previous research and compared Western European managers with Hungarian ones. What I really wanted to find out was the gap between how leaders were thinking, why they were thinking differently, and what results they got. To make it even more interesting, I divided the Hungarian managers into two categories: those who grew up and studied under communism and those who were affected by communism indirectly. The result of the research was shocking, and it contradicted everything I had read and learned about at the university. It turned out that **the gap between the two generations in Hungary was much bigger than the gap between the new generation and the Western Europeans**. This was not supposed to happen, as I knew, having passed exams discussing Hofstede, Trompenaars, and their theory about how culture was stable and country specific. But my data was clear: it wasn't true.

As we tend not to question models and solutions that have been around for forty years, I forgot about the results of my research and I started my first company.

The entrepreneurial rollercoaster

One night I was reading a book about the *Dragon's Den* (*Shark Tank* in the USA), the reality show featuring five millionaires who give entrepreneurs looking for investors three minutes to pitch their ideas. And a thought came to me, or maybe it was just hunger. I wanted to eat mussels, but I wasn't sure where to go. There were some obvious options (seafood restaurants), but there were so many places serving mussels, I was overwhelmed. Why could I not search for restaurants based on their live menus? It seemed like a great idea, so I made it happen. I created a website featuring 35 restaurants where people could search for, say, steak and get a list of results that enabled them to compare value by price, quality, and location. If users liked what they saw, they could click on the restaurant name and view the restaurant profile, where they could read the complete menu, the history of the place, an interview with the owner or head chef, and even download some recipes.

What did not occur to me at the time was restaurants often change their menus, sometimes on a daily basis. If a restaurant runs out of dishes and the menu isn't live, there is no point in using the website. So, I had to pivot and simplify the concept. I added booking functions and partnered with magazines, and a software company with fantastic digital products and IT resources. The joint venture seemed perfect. We grew the company to include 5,500 restaurants all over the UK, and I even signed a contract with OpenTable.

But then the perfect partnership turned into a living hell. I just could not work with the other CEO, who was French.

The Quest begins

Today I understand what happened, but at the time I did not. The situation just felt wrong and extremely stressful, and we ended up parting ways. The software company bought our shares, and we got out of the business. That's when I started my research again. How come I had years of experience, the partnership had been perfect on paper, my dissertation at Sussex had been on the very same topic, and yet I could not put theory into practice? Was it me or something else?

Instead of blaming someone, I wanted to understand what had gone wrong. I got certified in various intercultural, leadership and psychometric models to understand the blueprint of why people think and behave differently and how to turn those differences into synergy instead of painful liability. And I discovered why most programs fail so resoundingly despite the significant amount money and energy invested in them.

The result of that research is Global DISC™, the first intercultural behavioural model that **explains all three layers of identity, or WHAT, HOW, and WHY we think and feel the way we do.** It is an ICF-accredited, multi-award-winning solution used by Fortune 500 companies, national governments, local and global businesses to break down the barriers within and between people.

The purpose of this book is to share some of those findings, bust some urban legends in the intercultural and leadership field, and give you the latest, proven tools to recognise and understand the dynamics of individual and group mindset. Some of you may disagree with the ideas and concepts you read about here, which is perfectly normal. Keep an open mind and question why you disagree rather than dismissing it out of hand. My aim is not to convince you necessarily, but to get us to think together, and challenge and support each other, as it is very likely we are working towards similar goals.

Unfortunately, the natural human reaction is to assume when there's disagreement that we are right and the other person is wrong - and so our ultimate goal is to prove them wrong. The lesson I learned, and the basis for this book, is that it is highly unlikely somebody would claim to be right, unless they really think they are. In that case, it makes much more sense to ask them why they think so. What do they know that we don't? What can they see that we can't? Being able to ask these questions instead of reverting back to survival mode leads to innovation. That is where the potential is, and the key to unlocking it is developing our global mindset and becoming experts in the science of uncommon sense.

Global mindset

Nowadays we need to get a license for most things but not our mindset, which we use 24/7 and can be our greatest asset or liability in life. It is no surprise that using a tiny piece of a London map in Madrid is not going to be super helpful even if we listen to motivational speakers and think positive while trying harder to make it work. We'll just get lost more quickly. This pretty much sums up what we are doing when interacting with people. We use a tiny piece of our own mental map to make sense of why others think and behave the way they do. We tend to assume it is 100% and others have the same map. **Ninety-five per cent of our actions are based on unconscious bias stemming from values and beliefs we are not even aware of, and yet we assume we are logical and objective.**

Instead of trying to change others, we should get to know ourselves. The more we understand all three levels of our identity—what, how, and why we act, think, and feel the way we do—the more we are going to get along with others too. If we know who we are, we don't have to desperately cling onto external sources of identity such as nationality, profession, or job title. They are all part of us, true, but **culture is what we are used to, not who we are**.

Globalisation is merging cultures, alternative ways of living, working and existing, and different ideas of what common sense is. The dividing lines have become blurry, which scares many people. I am not minimising the importance of heritage (indeed, we need heritage to understand our journey), but our past should not be our future. Patriots understand the benefits and necessity of diversity, nationalists don't, and yet both groups 'know' they are right and their way is the only and proper way.

Even though trying to turn back the clock seems to be a trend, history clearly shows it is not a sustainable solution. Progress does not necessarily mean we get rid of the past; it means we keep what is valuable and look after it. At the same time, we have to let go of what isn't serving us anymore and replace it with what empowers us. That is the reason why I truly believe that **growth mindset is the foundation of global mindset, it is not an alternative to it.**

ICQ can help us to understand the difference and evolve as individuals and as a group. We have to learn from experience to create something better; otherwise, we're going to run into the same problems again and again on an even larger scale.

This is where ICQ is crucial. It is not about the statistically average values and beliefs of different countries but about the ability to see a situation from multiple perspectives so we can make better decisions. We are reluctant to change because changing implies something is wrong with us, but how about upgrading ourselves and our environment instead? **We are awesome, and we can be even better.**

We aren't born with our beliefs but we learn them, often subconsciously. Beliefs are rules created by individuals (others or us) and accepted and reinforced by a group. Belief is the feeling of certainty about something, a bunch of neurons in our brain created by thinking about something so many times it becomes automatic. It is merely a subjective interpretation of the outside world and if it does not empower us, it makes sense to change it for one we perceive to be better. That is something we all need in a stressful environment.

Putting a plaster on a problem won't fix it

Recent studies estimate stress is costing the economy over $300 billion a year in the USA alone. And, given the fact workplace stress is blamed for 120,000 deaths per year, how we cope with it can literally be a matter of life and death—and a huge determining factor in our health, happiness, and productivity. So how can we deal with it?

Let's assume we practice mindfulness every day, we decide to stay calm and carry on. We decide to be grateful for our job that comes with a wide range of entertainment and sometimes even useful employee benefits. Then we go to work, and our colleague, client, staff, or boss pisses us off by doing the same annoying thing they always do!

Nothing changed really: trying to treat the symptoms instead of fixing the root cause of a problem is never going to give you sustainable results.

Seventy-six per cent of 80 senior executives from 20 countries and 25 industries said the biggest barrier to long-term execution and strategy was employee interaction. In other words, people failing to work together to make things happen. (HBR, 2017)

In fact, 60–80% of all difficulties in organisations come from strained relationships among employees, and the three main causes of conflict are the clash of values and personalities under poor leadership. (Daniel Dana, Managing Differences, 2002)

Let's be honest. It does not matter how much we meditate or read about emotional intelligence. If we don't understand why another person behaves and thinks in a certain way, we might be able to restrain ourselves in the short term, but that is not going to solve anything in the long run.

People often generate explanations for other people's behaviours that align with stories they have previously constructed. They notice actions and attitudes that support these stories and overlook those that don't. As a result, their misperceptions—and the distrust, depression, and burnout they cause—endure and strengthen. This happens even though our stories are usually wrong in some way and we do not check them out before we act on them. Dr Gervase Bushe, author of

Clear Leadership: Sustaining Real Collaboration and Partnership at Work, calls this tendency "interpersonal mush".

Stress is not a disease but a state of mind that occurs when we feel we do not have the resources to cope with a situation and the picture in our head does not match reality. We expect other people to react and respond and then come to the same conclusion we have from a given set of 'facts' or 'circumstances' based on our own experience, expertise, and beliefs.

That is where variations of common sense are going to clash again and uncommon sense can help.

Before we move onto the next chapter, I need to explain the 'lord' header a few pages back. It is not a title given to me by the Queen, but a more commercial one thanks to British law. It is based on a historic English Lord of the Manor title that supports the legal right to use the honorific Lord or Lady if we own at least five square feet of dedicated estate land by Coniston Water within the Lake District National Park. That I do. It was the best ever Christmas present from my fiancée, Kasia. I probably won't change my name in my passport because, even though it would be completely legal, it would not make sense. Or would it?

CHAPTER 2

Busting the Myths of Cultural Intelligence

"Intelligent discontent is the mainspring of civilisation."
—Eugene V. Debs

The truth can set you free, but it will piss you off first.

Are you familiar with the Five Monkeys Experiment? A group of scientists placed five monkeys in a cage; in the middle of the cage was a ladder with bananas perched at the top. Every time a monkey went up the ladder, the scientists soaked the rest of the monkeys with cold water. After a while, whenever a monkey started up the ladder, the others pulled it down and beat it up. Eventually, none of the monkeys even tried climbing the ladder despite the temptation at the top.

The scientists then decided to replace one of the monkeys. The first thing the newcomer did was start to climb the ladder. Immediately, the others pulled him down and beat him up. After several beatings, the new monkey also learned never to go up the ladder, even though there was no evident reason not to, aside from the beatings.

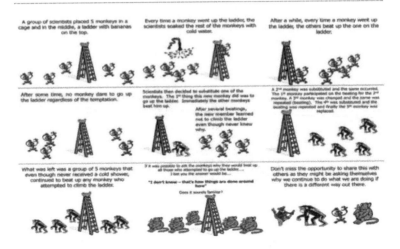

A second monkey was switched out and the same thing occurred: the first substitute participated in the beating of the second. When the third monkey was swapped out too, the same again. The fourth monkey was changed with the same results, and finally the fifth. What was left was a group of five monkeys that—without ever having received a cold shower—continued to beat up any monkey who attempted to climb the ladder. If it were possible to ask the monkeys why they beat up on all those who started climbing the ladder, their most likely answer would be, "I don't know. It's just how things are done around here."

Descriptions of this experiment have appeared many times in various blogs, books, and speeches, even though the experiment as described here never actually happened. The story originated with G.R. Stephenson's 1967 research into the learned responses of rhesus monkeys.

Why is this story relevant? Because we are still driven by very similar principles. If you go to YouTube and search for *Brain Games—Conformity (Waiting Room)*, you will find an eye-opening human version of an experiment that explains why social conformity is tremendously more powerful than most people realise.

This is the approach we see in the field of leadership and intercultural training. A lot of solutions exist. Some of them are

20

popular, and some of them are proven, although there is not much overlap within these categories.

For example, Myers-Brigg Type Indicator (MBTI) is one of the most popular psychometric tests. Over two million people use it every year even though 50% of them have a significantly different result when they take it five weeks later. (Fortune, 2013) This can be confusing, both for those who get a different result each time and for those who hope to understand themselves and others better by using the tool.

Companies are passionate about upgrading their technology and streamlining their process, yet there has hardly been any breakthrough in terms of understanding and leveraging diversity in the workforce. Are they using the same old tools because that's what they have always used or because they work? What costs more in the long run—investing in the latest solutions or sticking to the same old methods? Here are some recent numbers:

- 89% of hiring failures within the first 18 months are due to a poor cultural fit. Only 11% are due to lack of skills. (LeadershipIQ, 2016)
- 75% of employees leave managers not companies. (Gallup, 2016)
- 71% of surveyed organisations aspire to have an inclusive culture, but only 12% have achieved this objective. (Deloitte, 2016)
- 89% of CEOs *know* addressing leadership, culture, and engagement are the most urgent priorities. (Deloitte, 2016)

Business is about people and their mindset. Not knowing what we consider common sense before trying to figure out what common sense is to someone else can cause a business to fail.

Cultural intelligence is an increasingly well-known topic but a less clearly defined concept. Most people think about

21

statistically average national differences and workshops run by trainers who used to live abroad or academics who have written books about it. This is not a sarcastic comment, I qualify for both categories, too, and this section of the book is about sharing my insight about why that is not enough and why current people solutions do not deliver better results than the above-mentioned ones.

Myth #1 – Outdated solutions = outstanding results

Trying to fix a Smart TV with tools designed for a black-and-white one is not going to be particularly successful, if at all. If we wouldn't even try it, then why are outdated practices still used in the training industry?

Most intercultural models were created in the 1970s and 1980s based on the answers of people who grew up without the Internet, the European Union, or cheap flights. We do love our great grandparents, but we don't think or work like them. The world has changed a lot in the last thirty to forty years, and we face very different challenges that require new, updated solutions.

Over 90% of companies still buy and sell tools created in the last century. Whenever I have conversations with the CEOs of training and coaching organisations, I ask them if they have a lot of demand for cultural intelligence (ICQ) training. They usually say no. Then I ask if their company sells what the clients ask for, what they have in stock, or what the clients need. Customers usually ask for help when they are experiencing issues. And even then, they tend to talk about the symptoms only, or misdiagnose the actual root cause of the problem, or ask for something that might not help much.

If I go to my doctor, I consider it her/his responsibility to find out what the cause of my problem is and to recommend the best, most up-to-date solution instead of the one she/he used when she started her practice decades ago or the one that pays out the most commission. Likewise, if an accountant or a lawyer isn't familiar with the latest methods in their field, clients are probably going to take their business elsewhere. But that isn't the case in the coaching and training industry. The barrier of entry in this field is extremely low, which dilutes the market to such an extent it can be hard to tell the difference between coaches who studied and worked for years and those who just want to make money.

Myth #2 – Intercultural = international

The most popular intercultural models are about nationalities and their values. Some touch on generational differences or measure how sensitive people are in terms of noticing cultural differences. They are all useful tools, no doubt about it. They are perfect for the purpose they were designed for at that time. But the fact is, **80% of cultural differences exist within countries, not between them (HBR, 2016).** That's why we experience the 'millennial issue' or the gender gap. This being the case, how useful is it to learn about statistically average differences between nationalities?

As you can see from the culture wheel, each of us belongs to 10–20 cultural groups at once—education, generation, gender, profession, etc.—and they all influence our values and behaviour. Focusing on one cultural group alone and expecting

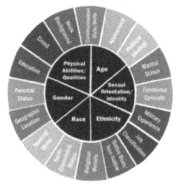

a long-lasting, impactful result is not realistic. Nationality and generation are probably the most well-known and easily disclosed categories, and therefore easy to pinpoint, but ignoring the others is like brushing your two front teeth only and expecting your mouth to be healthy.

Myth #3 – Statistically average country = statistically average individual

L. Todd Rose (co-founder and president of The Center for Individual Opportunity) had a fascinating TED Talk in 2013 where he talked about The Myth of Average.

During the 1950s, the US Air Force began thinking a lot about averages. At the time, pilots were having trouble controlling their planes. At first, the issue was pinned on pilot error and poor training. But the real problem turned out to be the cockpit itself or, more specifically, the fact the cockpit had just one design: it had been built for the average pilot in 1920s.

The Air Force concluded Americans had gotten bigger over the past couple of decades and all the service needed to do was to update the measurements of the average pilot. The Air Force measured more than 4,000 pilots on 10 dimensions of size that seemed important for fitting into a cockpit. The thinking was,

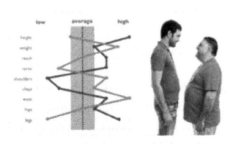

once they redesigned the cockpit for the average pilot of the 1950s, controlling the plane would no longer be an issue. They assumed most pilots would be within the average range in most dimensions and many would even be average in all ten.

How many were actually average?

Zero.

Even when just three dimensions of size were taken into account, fewer than 3.5 % of the pilots fell within the range defined as average.

Last-century intercultural models focused on the average results of a group, but what are the chances we'll meet a statistically average individual? It's true individuals conform to the norms of a group and those models can be useful when we move to a new country. But if our success depends on how well we understand the individuals we are dealing with, they can be very misleading and they can even backfire.

I often ask clients if they think they are statistically average examples of their nationalities. They hardly ever say yes. Then I ask them why they think other individuals would be. I fully agree it is crucial to learn about a country if we move there, because that knowledge can be helpful in understanding what the people there are used to, but it cannot tell us everything about them. The danger is we see what we anticipate. If I expect you to be a 'scientifically average' German, then that's what I am going to see even if you are not one, unless you act so differently that it catches me off guard and I have no idea what to do. This is why I am often sceptical about courses promising to explain how to deal with German employees or customers. If a course claims to describe what the 'normal' way of managing or serving groups of people in Germany is, that would be slightly more accurate and realistic. In the next chapter, I am going to share with you an interesting Fortune 500 company case study we did.

Our clients do not have a problem with a country; they have challenges with the individuals they have to lead, serve, or work with.

Myth #4 – More visible diversity = better results

Homophilic diversity is a strange-sounding concept that simply means we hang out with people who think like us even if they look very different. The word *homophily* comes from the Ancient Greek ὁμοῦ (homou, "together") and the Greek φιλία (philia, "friendship") and describes the tendency of individuals to associate and bond with others who are similar, as in the proverb, "Birds of a feather flock together". Homophily appears in a vast array of network studies. More than a hundred studies have observed homophily in some form or another and concluded similarity breeds connection, because common characteristics (beliefs, values, and education, for example) make communication and relationship formation easier.

Why is this important? Because it's the reason many intercultural and diversity and inclusion (D&I) initiatives might fail or cause more issues than they address. Most companies focus on the superficial layer of diversity (nationality, gender, generation, etc.), the layer with no proven benefit (Management International Review, 2016). What makes a real difference is **cognitive diversity**, the way someone thinks and processes information based on a different set of values, beliefs and experiences. There might be some overlap between the two layers, but more often than not there isn't, and we have plenty of case studies to prove that. **Diversity is cool until somebody disagrees with us.**

We like and trust people who are similar to us and/or who act and think in a familiar and predictable way. Imagine you are recruiting employees. Are you going to offer a job to

- somebody who looks like you but keeps disagreeing with you on every topic, or
- somebody who doesn't look at all like you, but the two of you hit it off immediately—or at least they don't make you feel everything you consider right is wrong?

Most people would go for the second option because doing so allows them to tick a lot of the right boxes, which means

- they could publish the statistics on their website proving they are a multicultural, open-minded, and inclusive company with x% of women, minorities, or nationalities, and
- the new hire could fit in perfectly, with no arguments or weird ways of doing things, and it would feel comfortable and familiar.

What's not to like? It sounds great! The benefits of diversity stem from its wide range of perspectives, which allows companies and people to see the same situation from several different angles and make better, more informed decisions. This is called **cognitive flexibility**. But that isn't the case here. On the surface, the team might seem to be diverse, but underneath they are very similar, hence the lack of proven benefit of that type of diversity. It's like having a fleet of similar cars in a wide range of colours.

Neuroscience confirms culture shock does not happen because we come up against architecture or traditions that are different from what we are used to. It happens because our brain is pushed out of its comfort zone. It no longer recognises the usual patterns and is forced to learn something new, which takes up too much energy. Our brain may be 2% of our body weight, but it uses 20% of our energy, which is why it is designed to create mental shortcuts (biases, habits) so it can run efficiently.

Cognitive diversity is uncomfortable and tiring, and it can be annoying, shocking, and frustrating. That is precisely why it gets us out of autopilot mode. If we can reframe the meaning of being uncomfortable so we realise it means we are getting stronger, smarter, and more adaptable, then we can significantly reduce our stress level while simultaneously increasing the amount of productivity and fun we experience.

Myth #5 – Incomplete approach = complete results

Behavioural models such as DISC (and its many different versions including those such as Insights Discovery that don't reference the DISC dimensions) are popular for a reason. Around 80% of Fortune 500 companies use them to help their employees connect with themselves and others (Shuchita Dua Dullu, 2017). They work. What those companies fail to consider is how culture (in this case environment) influences behaviour. It's fun to talk about different personality types, but how come these types behave similarly in a group? What are the underlying values and beliefs that drive the actual behaviour? When is personality stronger than peer pressure?

Psychometric models explain how different personality types tend to behave if they are not influenced by anyone or anything around them. There are not many situations like this, if any at all. Talking about personality types without ICQ is just half the complete package.

Myth #6 – More information = better skills

When I was a teenager I used to compete in ju-jitsu. I was the national champion at age 17, and I loved watching movies and instructional videos about martial arts. Eighteen years ago, I saw a documentary about different martial art experts—the best of the best in karate, kung fu, boxing, and so on—who were asked to fight a fully padded man. He was completely protected, so they could punch and kick him, no drama.

They put each contestant in a room with the padded man and then shouted, "Fight!" On cue the man started to scream and swear at them as he ran towards them. What happened? Some of the masters froze, and one of them even ran away. Why?

Because they were great within their environment and own style of martial arts, but when they got caught off guard and were faced with too many techniques, they had no idea what to do. The ones who did well were experts in martial arts such as Thai-boxing, boxing, or wrestling, which focus on fewer techniques practised over and over until they become instinctive.

This is what happens in the training industry as well. There is a workshop for everything, but usually just one. Statistics show we forget over 95% of what we learn within a month if we take notes. Retention is even less if we do not follow up.

The key is repetitive learning. Training in fewer techniques again and again so they become skills means we can focus on the task at hand instead of concentrating on the tool itself. **Theory without practice is like a tea bag without hot water**. The potential is there, we crave the end result, but it is not going to happen just like that.

Myth #7 - Golden Rule = connection with others

Do you believe in the Golden Rule? In treating people the way you want to be treated? When I ask this question during workshops, most people say yes. Me too. At least, from an ethical perspective I do. Otherwise it seems selfish. It would imply everybody is like us, they are motivated by what drives us, they even like whatever delights us.

Salesforce (the World's #1 CRM) asked hundreds of CEOs about their customer-service style and its level of satisfaction. Eighty per cent of them said it was outstanding. When they asked actual customers, only 8% of them agreed with them. That's a pretty huge gap. CEOs might think everybody likes what they do, but that is clearly not the case. What's key is to treat people the way they need and want to be treated, which is what US-based Dr Tony Alessandra coined the "Platinum Rule".

Just imagine the last time you were truly impressed as a customer. Probably you felt somebody read your mind. They knew what you expected so they could exceed your expectations and wow you. Chances are you were being helped by someone who was being managed by a leader who understood what drove that employee and could create a motivating environment around that person.

Employees treat our business the way we treat them. Our intention might be good, and we might assume more money or a promotion can improve performance, but from an employee's perspective that might mean uncertainty and more pressure, and they'll just want extra days off instead.

Myth #8 - Smart individuals = high-performing team

The average life expectancy of most CEOs is now somewhere between thirty and forty months. CEOs face more challenges than ever today as the complexity of business continues to grow. Business is changing rapidly, and CEOs need to be ahead of the curve.

Innovation has become a critical goal for many companies. There is, however, a fundamental dilemma that comes with innovation. Many companies want innovation but aren't tolerant of mistakes. They can't have it both ways. Innovation requires both a psychologically safe environment and exceptional leaders who can bring out the best in employees with outstanding skills and diverse perspectives.

When companies put smart people in teams, they are hoping to create synergy by combining their skills; in reality, those differences turn into liability. **On average, 79% of performance is lost because of clashing values and personalities combined with poor leadership.** All three reasons stem from the same source: a lack of understanding of the blueprint of why people think and behave differently. Once companies do understand, they can focus on what they want to achieve instead of fighting what they don't.

The fact is, most leadership models are based on the research and experience of North American and Western European academics and businesspeople. However, most of the world thinks and behaves rather differently. This is not to say there are no universal principles. What I mean is, leadership is about being competent and confident in most situations, so having a wide range of perspectives and behavioural styles combined with real self-awareness is the key to levelling up. According to Marshall Goldsmith, the only two-time Thinkers 50 #1 Leadership Thinker in the world, 70% of his clients believe they are in the top 10% of their field. It is highly likely most of them are incorrect about their own performance.

In today's fast-moving, complex organisations, 90% of execution is interaction between people who think and behave differently. The skill to turn those differences into synergy is the key to remaining competitive. The more we understand why people think and behave differently, the better it is for our business.

It is a common misconception that seemingly homogeneous teams have fewer issues, as a company called 3circlepartners in the USA discovered. They gave an assessment to each member of a team, scored them individually, and then had the team submit a second assessment collectively. We can see the result below. The blue dots are the group result, and the green ones are the best possible individual scores. It's clear there is a significant gap between the potential of the team and their actual results. They repeated the research several times and found the average gap was 79%. That is how much potential a team loses when we expect to create synergy by combining their skills.

Measuring the Interaction Gap

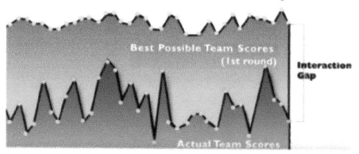

"Close the interaction gap" by Max Isaac and Anton McBurnie

The question is: What's the percentage in your company? Is it 40% or 80%? **Cultural differences are like corporate diabetes, the silent killer. The symptoms are invisible for a long time, and when they become apparent, it might be too late.** Leaders tend to believe they do not need intercultural training if they don't have an international team. The fact is, they do. **If they employ or serve more than one person, they are multicultural already even if they are not multinational.** On the other hand, a typical country-specific training would not really benefit them nor would a personality-based one explain the dynamics of individual and group mindset.

Let's go deeper into the topic of ICQ by discussing the underlying reason for its existence, the diversity of people.

CHAPTER 3

Beyond the Rainbow

"Diversity is being invited to the party; inclusion is being asked to dance."

—Verna Myers

The title of the chapter might trigger some negative reaction for the wrong reason, a few minutes later it is going to be clear what it refers to. The example under the title is a common metaphor used to highlight the difference between diversity and inclusion, which some people assume are synonymous. The quote has a nice ring to it, but it fails to address **the missing link, the issue of low self-esteem, or lack of self-inclusion.**

The term *inclusion* seems to be everywhere nowadays. If you google the word, chances are the search turns up rainbow-coloured graphics of people, puzzles, and trees, and a very long list of links to articles on the subject. And yet, despite all the energy and money being invested in this area, everyday life shows little improvement which is even more reflected in the current political climate.

Why is the concept of inclusion so difficult to put into practice? The more I research the topic—and diversity, culture, and mindset—the clearer it becomes to me most approaches focus on the symptoms rather than the root cause of its challenges.

I believe the main issue is low self-esteem. Put simply, what we think of others depends on how well we think of ourselves. Having low self-esteem makes us feel we don't measure up to other people or their expectations. People with good self-esteem don't depend on external validation: they know who they are, and most importantly, they are okay with it. If we already accept ourselves, we don't have to throw our weight around or hide away to feel safer.

"On", the other hand, if somebody lacks self-esteem, they often display aggressive behaviour, such as bullying, to make themselves feel good or at least better.

It is nearly impossible to be aggressive without feeling threatened. I've seen that countless times in martial art classes. The loudest, scariest-looking guys never scared me. I know they had a lot to compensate for, and I quickly found out what that was so I could use it against them. The ones who arrived on the scene quietly, but looked into everybody's eyes, were the ones to watch out for. **They had nothing to hide, nothing to prove. That is real confidence.**

Bringing other people down gives bullies a false feeling of self-confidence. We can see this type of behaviour at work and in politics. **The more uncertainty people face, the more stress they experience, and the more they revert to survival mode, which is certainly not inclusive.** When we perceive a situation or person as intimidating, our reptilian brain kicks in. We don't have to be friendly or smart—we have to be quick and strong. Low self-esteem is a widespread mental affliction that has reached epidemic proportions. The highly deceptive nature of social media created an immense illusion of gap between our normal and the new, seemingly insanely higher level of normal around us. It allows (or maybe forces?) us to compare the real or made-up highlights of others to our lowest and darkest feelings. The more deprived we feel, the more we crave something and the lower our self-esteem goes if we are not in control of our own mindset.

Only when we start with **self-inclusion** can we fully include others. But not until then.

The more we understand our own mindset, the more credibility we earn with ourselves, the more skills we acquire, the more confident we become, then the less we project our fears and insecurities onto others.

For example, let's imagine you invite me to a party and once we get there you ask me to dance. I would be really grateful, but I would politely say no. "It's not you, it's me" is such a cheesy way of brushing off somebody, but in this case it would be true. I would love to say yes, but I can't because I'm bad at dancing. I would find it embarrassing to step on you or miss 87% of the beats. You have the best of intentions, you are being as inclusive as possible, and yet your attempt at inclusivity still seemingly fails. If I make things worse by not being brave enough to tell you why I've refused, you might interpret my reaction based on my behaviour alone and conclude I am antisocial, cold, boring, rude, awkward or I might even have a problem with you.

Inclusion, like leadership, starts with us. **If we cannot lead ourselves, we struggle to lead others.** Either we aren't strong enough or we overcompensate because of our insecurities and inability to trust.

What's more, without inclusion first, diversity can cause more trouble than benefit. Companies proudly aim to be more visibly diverse because it is supposed to be good for business. In theory, it is true, but management needs to know the difference between diversity and inclusion.

Discussion is as often mistaken for argument as inclusion is for diversity

Have you ever been to IKEA to buy a piece of furniture? Most people have, and it's a weird experience. You check the brochure or the display, and you fall in love with a wardrobe. You jot down the number, go to the till and order it, and then you get a flat pack.

You go home excited and begin assembling it according to the instructions. If you're like me, you ignore them because nobody can tell you what to do, you know how to assemble it anyway, and it can't be that difficult with your skills and experience. Two hours later, you might realise it isn't that simple, there are more or fewer pieces than needed (suspicious, isn't it?), you have had enough, and you have come to the conclusion flat packs are a stupid idea: they don't work.

This is where the IKEA experience costs us a significant amount of money. **Relying on common sense and previous experience is not enough to turn diversity into inclusion. Diversity is the equivalent of the different pieces on the floor with a lot of potential to become a dream wardrobe. Inclusion corresponds to all those parts fitting together, supporting one another, and transforming into a stunning piece of furniture.**

The process is quite similar in companies. It's the difference between lots of people working independently and unsure of what they should be doing next, and a successful mix of people who work in harmony, creating synergy and superior performance.

The question I often get from CEOs and HR people is: "How can we create inclusion if all people are unique and there are so many cultures in the world?"

It's possible if company leaders focus on finding the similarities first, so they can build a common ground and learn how to make the most of the differences. If they do not understand their own and other people's strengths and weaknesses, values and beliefs, they can never create an inclusive environment.

Investing in people is not a luxury but rather the bare minimum with the highest ROI a company can spend money on.

Here's an example. A hotel department has five employees in a shift, but as business is pretty quiet and they want to save money, they send two people home. They save £15–20 an hour. A motivated and skilled staff could sell the multiple of that amount, or they could come up with insights and ideas to make even more profit. If management listened to them and if those employees felt valued and motivated. This is a typical example we see in failing companies and the exact opposite of what we see in successful ones. Eighty-five per cent of success is down to people skills, which are worth learning because treating people the way they want to be treated is very profitable. Cultural intelligence (ICQ) is the highest form of soft skills. But there's a catch.

How is diversity good for business?

Do you remember the devices on the left? They were common in the 1970s and 1980s, and you probably had most of them or at least something similar. At the time they were the latest technology, but today's equivalents would be very different. The knowledge and expertise that was enough to use and fix the older devices would not be enough for the latest versions today.

In fact, a quantum leap has happened recently and most of those devices can be replaced with a smartphone. The smartphone is popular because developers and engineers have managed to seamlessly integrate all those functions into one portable, user-friendly device. The technology behind it is complicated, but as end users we love the device for its apparent simplicity and ability to make our lives easier.

What if we collected all those different devices in the picture and put them together in a box? Would they turn into a smartphone? Would they function like one? Not really. Unfortunately, that is what most companies try to do: **they employ a diverse range of excellent people and then teach them how to be 'normal' while expecting to create synergy**

37

and make the team work like a smartphone. That is not going to happen, as we've seen.

Companies hear about the potential business case and also understand they have to be politically correct, so they start employing people from a wide range of cultural backgrounds. Then problems start emerging: misunderstandings, arguments, frustration, high staff turnover, decreased productivity, confusion. In the worst case, lawsuits and legal action.

What happened? Diversity seemed to be so tempting and simple in the news. Where is the potential it promised?

As we discussed in the previous chapter, nowadays diversity is dealt with on the superficial level and focuses on identity differences such as gender, generation, nationality, and so on. This approach has no proven benefit. As researchers Alison Reynolds, of the Ashridge Business School, and David Lewis, a director at the London Business School, discovered, **the kinds of diversity we most commonly think of—gender, race, age— have no correlation to a team's performance** (*Harvard Business Review*, 2017). Again, what does make a difference is cognitive diversity, or whether team members have different perspectives and different styles of processing knowledge. The challenge with cognitive diversity, up to now, has been the difficulty in measuring it and publishing the numbers on websites.

Here I must clarify my last statement to avoid misunderstanding. I am not suggesting we should ignore the visible layer of diversity. The fact leaders tend to prefer employees who are more similar to them is a real problem. It's simply wrong that women don't get paid the same salary as men for the same work. It's unfair that our name can determine whether we get a job interview or not. Tackling issues such as gender and race (to name but two) is important, and the approach I'm talking about here isn't instead of but in addition to.

There continues to be another challenge though. Even if a team is cognitively diverse, that alone does not guarantee a good result. What's required is a level of ICQ, or how much the team can leverage their personal and cultural differences.

If cognitive diversity is what we need to succeed in dealing with new, uncertain, and complex situations, we need to encourage people to reveal and deploy their different modes of thinking. We need to make it safe to try things multiple ways. This means leaders will have to get much better at building their team's sense of psychological safety.

There is much talk of authentic leadership, i.e., being yourself. Perhaps it is even more important that leaders focus on enabling others to be themselves.

When people don't get along, the problem isn't incompatibility—it is usually inflexibility _and_ lack of self-awareness, in other words, ICQ. Diversity offers the potential for, not a guarantee of, success. If somebody gave me all the parts for an airplane, I would not be able to put it together, so the different pieces would not add much value to my life. I could assume the pieces are worthless and airplanes don't fly. I could blame the media for promising a wide range of metal pieces would allow me to fly, but the truth is it would be my responsibility to acquire the knowledge to make the most of what I had.

Companies realise they need to motivate their workforce, so they spend a fortune on employee engagement and well-being programs. But, like a spa treatment, this approach is not going to solve the problem: it deals with symptoms only. When employees go back to work and discover they still cannot stand their colleagues, they find the clients irritating, and they are unable to handle their boss, they become even more upset and stressed. If we have a headache, we can take a painkiller to make it go away; however, that won't solve the problem if we are dehydrated or have a more serious health issue.

Engagement is closely related to self-esteem, inclusion, and how much we understand the science of uncommon sense.

Making employees happy is pure luxury

But making employees feel fulfilled is a moral obligation. That's what companies should aim for. What's the difference?

Seeking happiness isn't wrong, it's just limiting. It's only one colour on the rainbow of human experience. Contrary to popular belief, life is not about being happy. Don't get me wrong: happiness is important because it allows us to drop into and experience the pleasure of being alive, the joy of the moment. By all means, let's do things that bring us joy and happiness. But bear in mind happiness is merely an emotional state: fleeting, temporary, and elusive.

Fulfilment, on the other hand, is persistent and offers the full range of emotional experiences. For instance, we can be unhappy or stressed and yet very fulfilled. Indeed, being unhappy or stressed can be an essential part of fulfilment.

"The best moments in our lives are not the passive, receptive, relaxing times... The best moments usually occur if a person's body or mind is stretched to its limits in a voluntary effort to accomplish something difficult and worthwhile."

—Mihaly Csikszentmihalyi

Being in the flow means we are so involved in a task we lose track of time and space. It requires the right amount of challenge (stress) and the right number of skills. One too many might lead to anxiety and panic, but too few would leave us bored. The experience of flow is universal. It occurs across different classes, genders, ages, and cultures, and it can be experienced in many types of activities.

If you've ever experienced flow, then you've experienced some of its great benefits. When you're immersed in your chosen activity, you have a purpose. You're also free from worries about the past or the future as you turn your attention to only the present moment. And you even fine-tune your craft during your immersion—you know what they say, "Practice makes perfect." Okay, technically it isn't true. Practice makes an activity a habit; it makes it permanent. If you practice the wrong move, you are going to be very good at it, but it won't make what you're doing perfect.

Most employee engagement programs offer instant gratification packaged as tiny happiness tokens in the hope of improving productivity and overall morale at work. The real solution is to understand what drives those employees, so they can create a motivating environment where they can get into the flow. It is about making them feel understood and fulfilled. That is the sustainable solution, while aiming for happiness only is temporary.

Leadership is not about making everyone happy but about taking responsibility for providing the right amount of challenge and support simultaneously. Competition and disagreement are essential for growth. Diversity provides plenty of opportunities for both. Even though different perspectives often clash, ICQ can turn those differences into synergy instead of painful liability before they rip the teams and their future apart.

When we have a disagreement with someone, what is our first thought? What is our strategic objective? There are politically correct answers and there are real ones. It does not matter how much we practice and understand ICQ—instincts are strong, and most of us want to be right and come out of the situation as a winner as quickly as possible. That is a normal reaction. A constructive response would be the willingness to learn more about the other person's perspective and come up with a solution together that is better than either originally suggested.

That is how diversity is packaged. So much potential, but nobody told us how difficult it is going to be. When I was a teenager, I bought a lot of gadgets to sculpt my body into the shape of Greek statues of gladiators (not my best case study: never happened). My assumption was buying the latest, most advanced devices and supplements would guarantee my success. I paid for them, so I deserved to look good. That logic kept me a half-finished sculpture of an Olympic athlete because I did not put the required amount of work and consistency into my project. Diversity is pretty similar. It is the potential, and it is real, but it needs a lot of work and the mastery of uncommon sense. Good intention is not enough.

Celebrating diversity is as useful as sending good thoughts to disaster victims

It's well meant, but it doesn't do much. At least not for the people who actually need help.

Updating our Facebook profiles with the flag of the country where the latest tragedy happened is barely enough to make ourselves feel better by showcasing what caring people we are. It looks good on our website and social media, it projects empathy to our audience, but it doesn't really help anybody.

The alternative? The willingness and ability to make a real difference by actively contributing to the solution. This requires sacrifice and energy but is the most rewarding path even if we do not make it public.

Recently I've noticed a trend. Politicians, CEOs, and celebrities all make a lot of noise when something bad happens, but only a few take action that benefits others as well as themselves. For example, according to church and business officials, as of July 2019, the French billionaires who publicly proclaimed they would give hundreds of millions to rebuild Notre-Dame had not paid a penny towards the restoration of their national monument. Instead, it was mainly American and French individuals, via Notre-Dame's charitable foundations, who were behind the first donations, paying the bills and salaries for up to 150 workers employed by the cathedral since the April 15 fire devastated its roof and caused its magnificent spire to collapse.

Getting publicity was good for the billionaires, but the real heroes were those who actually acted but received no real recognition.

Diversity is such a hot topic nowadays everybody wants to be part of the visible, superficial layer to show the world how many women, nationalities, and disabled people they employ.

Three things are wrong with this approach:

- **These companies tend to aim for diversity, not inclusion**. Employing them does not necessarily mean they have equal opportunities or employees are actively engaged.
- **They tend not to focus on cognitive diversity**, the invisible, deeper layer that can make or break a team and the overall business.
- **They tend to believe diversity on its own is going to be good for business**, although they do not invest in ICQ programs to make it work as they might not be aware how much it is needed.

A recent article has sparked a debate about an ICQ conference full of white, middle-aged men. People were outraged by the lack of visible diversity. No one ever considered all those people had different experience, expertise, upbringing, personality types, etc. Just because we can't see it, does it mean it doesn't exist?

This topic can blow up conversations. **People feel so passionate about their own approach to ICQ, it gives them the kind of tunnel vision they usually fight against**.

Last time I had a conversation about this topic was with a fellow intercultural coach, who got upset and sent me a series of emails about white privilege and racism. I was surprised, as my update on LinkedIn had nothing to do with this topic, but it turned out she thought I had stated homogenous groups offered more benefit than diverse ones. I didn't know how she understood that, but I explained cognitive diversity is *not instead of* any other type of differences. It is an often overlooked part of the issue, something that should not be ignored.

The actual conversation was not too constructive because the other coach labelled it a "battle" and refused to talk over the phone. The ability to hold a dialogue with people who have different perspectives is the key to making progress. In this case, we were even on the same side, and I still could not change her initial judgement. I do not advocate for ignoring identity differences; indeed, I am all for it. That is why I believe **ignoring the deep layer of diversity can never yield complete solutions,** because the lack of results might make people think diversity is not good for business at all. This would be the real tragedy. **It is like investing in a high-end laptop and then sending it back, claiming I was unable to check emails or browse the Internet when the real problem was I did not know how to connect to the Wi-Fi.**

Having said that, I have also had a slightly different experience where my proposal was rejected because it was a "just another intercultural model created by a white man". It is not a joke, that was the exact sentence used when they discussed the meeting in private my friend attended, too. The shocking part is that the person who said it was a leader in an organisation specialised in promoting diversity. Judgements and assumptions can come from every angle, biases span across all cultural groups.

Later on, I am going share some case studies where we measured the cognitive diversity index of a seemingly truly diverse group and they turned out to be surprisingly similar inside.

Being similar inside while expecting to be different can turn into a self-fulfilling prophecy and the perceived differences can rip a team apart. The following story is a positive example of how cognitive diversity can also be useful.

Some years ago, I had the fortune to work with global CEOs and their international teams who seemed to have problems mostly based on misunderstandings. They had already tried typical intercultural training that focused on national differences based on the average result of thousands of assessments completed by a generation that grew up without the Internet.

44

It only widened the gap. Trying the same thing again and expecting different results is the definition of insanity, so they invested in the latest approach at ICQ Global.

During our workshop, we realised over 90% of the group had similar profiles and underlying drivers despite the fact the participants came from five different countries. That was when they understood how much the team had in common and how they could make the most of their differences. They all had similar needs and values, and they applied different best practices to meet those needs and achieve those goals.

Sending people on courses and making them do online programs is pretty much waste of money. It doesn't amount to much more than a nice gesture unless the senior leadership is fully committed and they know exactly why they have to participate. Then magic happens, because people are inspired and have faith in their company. That is the alternative: the willingness and ability to make a real difference by actively contributing to the solution.

That organisation is in the top half of Fortune 500 companies. Their people are their competitive advantage, not just in their mission statement but in real life as well.

Diversity is all around us; inclusion is often the missing part. I may own a hundred books, but they won't make me smarter if I do not read them and consciously apply the knowledge I learn. The world has changed more in the last thirty to forty years than in the 150 years prior, so how can we expect outdated people solutions to deliver the results they once promised?

If they cannot, how come corporate training is slow to change? Isn't it time to take a deeper look at the interconnection between diversity and inclusion?

Adults learn through massive trauma

Adults who run businesses might think learning is uncomfortable until they realise it is the only way to avoid a painful failure.

Since the year 2000, over 50% of Fortune 500 companies have been replaced because they held the false belief the future is just a slightly modified version of the present. **Complex problems require diverse perspectives.**

According to *The New Yorker*, 2017 was the year of diversity fatigue, a concept I agree with. Great ideas and concepts lose value when people turn them into PR stunts and fancy corporate fads.

Forcing diversity at the expense of inclusion has created a situation where existing members of a group feel ignored, scared, and disengaged. The intention might be good, but without the right skills and knowledge, **without inclusion, diversity turns into liability.** From now on, we should focus on leveraging personal and cultural differences instead of riding the PR wave of 'the more diverse we are, the cooler we look'.

The point is not to employ the full range of skin colours, sexual orientations, and nationalities, but to create a psychologically safe and empowering environment where people with a wide range of perspectives and background can fulfil their potential, challenge the status quo, and drive innovation.

In fact, we need to strive for inclusion *before* trying to be more diverse. The challenge, according to the pre-2000 approach to diversity of visible traits, is if we look different, we must be different inside as well. That is certainly not the case, and we have plenty of examples to prove it. One day I had a meeting with a consultant who worked for one of the Big 4, during which he perfectly summed up the situation: "It must cost a fortune for companies to recruit employees from all over the world who think just like them."

Although deep, cognitive diversity is still invisible, today it is possible to measure it and publish the numbers on websites. Our research has clearly proven even our family members can be more different than somebody on the other side of the globe. We may have learned how to behave 'normally', but this does not mean we have similar values and beliefs. The goal is not just to create the complete spectrum, but to develop the ICQ mentality of being and, in case of disagreement when different perspectives clash, the ability to ask the right questions:

- What does the other person know I do not?
- What can the other person see I cannot?

Sound obvious? Well, in theory it might be. In real life it looks like this:

- I am right, he must be wrong, I have to prove it.
- What if she is right? I would look stupid! I cannot let it happen!

Yes, it's easier to have people around us who are like us, but that won't get us far at all. It's a no-brainer determining which is more efficient: a football team with 11 different players who have learned how to leverage their skills or a team with 11 goal keepers.

Diversity is the mixture of differences; **inclusion** is the right mixture of people managed with ICQ. One is a minefield and other one is a gold mine.

Locker room talk and mission statements

When a topic is both important and trendy—and diversity and inclusion is a prime example—employees often talk about it like teenagers talk about sex.

"Of course, I do it! I am the best at it! What about you?"

"Me? You have no idea … even better!"

Usually this is a lie, no matter how much they want to believe it.

Job candidates love powerful mission statements around company culture, because they can also position themselves as the perfect match for the opportunity. Then everybody can keep up appearances for a while. But there is a limit, and the truth about incompatibility will surface. The wrong hiring decision can have a huge impact on the performance of the team. In fact, an organisation can be looking at a cost of up to 2.5 times the individual's salary. The disruption overall business can be considerable as well.

Cultural fit is the glue that holds an organisation together. That's why it's key to identify and clarify it. Even before the hiring team starts recruiting, they need to be able to define and articulate the organisation's values, goals, and practices and then weave this understanding into the hiring process.

According to some professionals, culture can be hard to define and difficult to measure. But in my view, it is not that hard: it is behaviour that is rewarded or punished. **Asking people what they value and agree with is very different from asking them what they would do in a certain situation.** Most people value health and agree it is important, and yet they go home to a cigarette, a pint of beer, and a pizza. The difference between the two approaches is like the difference between a Tinder profile picture and what the person actually looks like.

The question is, what happens if we use our corporate Tinder profile (fancy mission statements, powerful values, smiling employees on the website) and new hires fall for it? According to LeadershipIQ, 89% of new hires leave within 18 months due to poor cultural fit. The reason is not that they are not good enough, but something else. From the company perspective, they were the wrong candidates; from the (ex-) employees' point of view, the company was untruthful because the norms (what actually goes on in the organisation) seriously clashed with the values they tried to project.

Would it make sense to measure values based on actual behaviour and use the same framework to objectively measure the intercultural gap between groups and individuals? The next chapter explains what diversity without ICQ can result in on both a personal and corporate level.

CHAPTER 4

Misunderstanding: The Biggest Distance Between Two People

"The single biggest problem in communication is the illusion that it has taken place."
— George Bernard Shaw

Assumptions are to communication what termites are to wood.

Termites can cause serious damage in the wooden structure of a house and go undetected for a long time. In an average year, termites are responsible for $1–$2 billion in property damage in the USA alone. The destruction they cause is usually evident before they are.

Sound familiar? Everything seems to be fine with our company, our relationship, our family, or our customers, and then things start to fall apart. Familiarity can be dangerous. Staying in our comfort zone can turn into laziness or create a stronger pattern of assumptions that can spread into new relationships and situations.

How many times do we make assumptions about what people like or do not like? Or how they will react to an event or something we need to tell them? Or even what they are thinking, what motivates them, what their desires are? If we all worked on the assumption what we accept as true is *really* true, there would be little hope of advancement and innovation. Expectations are usually not productive. If somebody doesn't live up to our expectations, we're disappointed; if they do, we feel nothing much because things turned out as we expected. There is no positive upside to it.

No matter how open we think we may be, preconception— or bias—affects all of us. According to the research conducted by the Perception Institute, 85% of Americans consider themselves to be without bias. In fact, all of us carry biases that exist and operate beneath our conscious awareness. We do 95% of our mental processing in our unconscious mind. And that is where we collect and store our implicit biases.

We need to challenge what we believe about ourselves. In addition to gender and sexuality, we also need to talk about race, religion, age, and all forms of diversity, which has the potential to enrich our personal and professional lives. This is where ICQ becomes important, for individuals and big companies alike. It is the foundation of self-development.

According to Gallup, 72% of leaders believe they are outstanding, although 82% of their employees say they are uninspiring. That's an enormous gap between perception and actual impact. Why is that? How can we bridge the gap?

We can only improve if we know what our weaknesses and blind spots are. By weakness I do not mean we are not good enough at something. I'm referring to understanding we are subconsciously influenced by our cultural background, and our brain processes and fits all new information into an existing system so it seems logical and reasonable. We do not even consider the possibility of being wrong because we see only what we know. **But what if the information we dismiss could save our business or give us a breakthrough idea?**

Unconscious bias—the misunderstood friend

Unconscious bias is like Google's 'I'm feeling lucky' function: we quickly find what we're looking for. Most of us are quite happy about this option, because it saves time and hassle and has the bonus of making us feel smart.

It raises a few questions, though.

- Do we understand the algorithm that produced the result?
- Would searching for something slightly different produce a very different result?
- Is the result true or just something that satisfies our point of view?
- Would we have found a more accurate result if we had checked a wider range of options?
- Do we want to be right, or do we actually want to learn and find the real answer?

The old joke about the looking for lost car keys under the streetlamp because it's dark everywhere else plays out all too often in today's landscape of big data. It's human nature to want to be right and to prove we are in a way that can't be challenged.

Our biases are influenced by our background, cultural environment, and personal experiences, and they have enormous impact on what we consider to be true and logical. Even if we refuse to admit it, our first impressions of people seldom change. The reason is not necessarily our expertise in understanding people, but the way our brain subconsciously links the person to something we know or have experienced in the past. This is known as **cognitive bias**, a mental shortcut that allows us to make quicker decisions, save energy, and keep ourselves safe. Fighting it is like trying to get rid of our eyesight. Both exist for a reason. The key is to understand how they work

51

and how we can make them more accurate and empowering. In both cases, we want to see more clearly.

One example of unconscious bias are stereotypes. The definition of the word *stereotype* is "...a fixed, overgeneralised belief about a particular group or class of people" (Cardwell, 1996). The term derives from the Greek words στερεός (stereos, "firm, solid") and τύπος (typos, "impression"), hence "solid impression".

During ICQ Global workshops, I ask participants to look at the picture below and write down the subjects' nationality, profession, and three other things about them that come to mind.

Usually the participants decide the blonde is Swedish or Russian. Some like her; others think she is cold, smart, or heartless. They often conclude the lady in the middle is a student or journalist from Brazil, and the gentleman at top right a tattoo artist or Hell's Angel.

In fact, the blonde is what Facebook decided I would look like if I had been born as a woman. Some of the participants are surprised by this, especially the ones whose first impression was exceptionally pleasant and adventurous. The reason I show them this photo is because learning is an emotional process. The more intense the experience, the more people remember it. Plus, it's a really good picture.

Successful people challenge themselves and are eager to learn. That is the foundation of cultural intelligence (ICQ). It isn't about looking at the dos and don'ts in different cultures but about understanding ourselves first before trying to understand others. **Culture is NOT a synonym for countries. Learning about them based on data from the last century is as much cultural intelligence as eating broccoli with a steak and calling ourselves vegetarian.**

ICQ: the science of personal achievement

ICQ is about connecting with ourselves and others by learning to see the world from different perspectives. Instead of relying on our 'feeling lucky' function, we make the effort to explore different ways of searching and check different results. ICQ starts with us. If we don't know how our minds work, what drives our behaviour, and how we can get out of our own way, we seriously limit our potential. Everything supports this. **Breakthroughs come as a result of shifting our commitment from the predictable future (comfort zone) to one with more potential (discomfort zone). The problem is our brain is not designed to do that. If we want to push past our limits and carve out the person we are capable of being, then we need to go against nature, because our brain is going to try to talk us out of it.** The more we understand the brain's processes, the more control we gain and the further we can go.

Let's see how our brain works.

If you are a neuroscientist, then you might disagree with the claim we have three brains, and you would be right. I use the number intentionally to make the topic as practical and understandable as possible while keeping it accurate.

The three brains are an evolutionary adaptation, and all of them have separate functions. Imagine a car has three drivers. Only one can drive, and all the other two can do is influence the driver. They can swap seats anytime, but still, only one can be in charge. That's why it is important to recognise and understand who is in control and how we can influence them.

The **reptilian brain** pays attention to a very few things only. First of all, it evaluates whether something is an opportunity or a threat, either physical or emotional. If something is perceived as a danger, then the reptilian brain kicks in. Its function is to ensure the survival of the individual, and it responds only in three ways: fight, flee, or freeze.

Nowadays ideally there is no physical danger, so how can we recognise when our reptilian brain is at work? We feel it when we are stressed. The fleeing mode manifests as anxiety, the fight mode as aggression, the freeze mode as helplessness.

The **limbic brain** is concerned with the survival of the group. From an evolutionary perspective, it seems logical. Living in groups is safer provided the group is stable. That stability requires a structure to determine the group's different roles.

How can we tell the limbic brain is in control? People become territorial. They try to impress or intimidate us. The good news is this function is not about fighting but about trying to. Usually someone tries it three or four times to test the water and then disengages. Think of fights that occur in the animal kingdom. An animal rarely kills another if it's from the same herd because that's not the goal. Between other herds and species, though, it can be an entirely different story.

The limbic brain is our autopilot and we use it 95% of the time. We store all our memories here. It recognises patterns and situations, and processes and issues instructions. It saves us time and energy because we do not have to focus on basic tasks.

The limbic brain is responsible for raw emotions and personality types with two different layers of motivation:

- **Intrinsic:** responds to whatever gives us joy and energy. This determines how we want to behave and who we are.
- **Extrinsic:** responds to our environment, for example, social expectations (the blueprint of how we should behave). Usually these types of motivation are not sustainable as they require energy from us and fade if not successful. Nonetheless, extrinsic motivation can be the stronger of the two.

If we understand someone's intrinsic motivation, we can influence them to achieve a win-win situation. If we appeal to their extrinsic needs, then there will be regrets later on, because it's a temporary solution only. For instance, do we do our job because it makes us fulfilled or pays us well? If we do it just for the money, we will need a regular pay rise to satisfy that need; otherwise, we will be frustrated and angry.

When we use our limbic brain, we become resistant to change and cannot see opportunity. The limbic brain rejects new ideas and looks for social order and hierarchy instead. Who is this person? Do they represent power and authority? Do they know what they are talking about? Can I trust them? If the answer is yes, then the message gets passed into the neocortex.

The **neocortex** is the analytical brain, and it is logical. A deciding factor regarding how a message is perceived is how easy it is to understand and process. It is believed to be the primary location of human thought, including the ability to form ideas and feelings into words. In mice, monkeys, and humans, its basic building blocks (neurons) are the same, and it has a similar six-layer structure. However, the human cortex is by far the largest: 10 times the surface area of the monkey's and 1,000 times that of the mouse. It makes us adaptable, helps us to make better decisions, and drives us to become more successful, creative, and in control.

The challenge is how to connect with and influence different personality types, all with their own perception of danger, opportunity, and incentive, in the most efficient way. Relying on common sense and good intention would imply everybody is like us, which is wildly untrue. Rather than being universal, preferences are as subjective as the people who have them.

Our unconscious mind helps us manage human relationships. It relies on schema (selections of meanings we use to interpret a situation) and script (expected behaviour in a particular context). This is what culture is based on. It is a network of shared meaning, a set of unwritten rules we need to follow in order to be accepted. **To put it simply, culture is a cognitive bubble where most things make sense.**

This network is the deep layer of culture. It is less visible as it works in the background, guiding our interactions and providing us with interpretive frameworks for looking at things. It gives us an intuitive sense of what is normal and expected, and it acts like a glue for shared habits and standards. That is why travelling can be stimulating, stressful, and transformative all at once.

Globalisation has seemingly diluted the intercultural experience (for instance, Starbucks seems to be everywhere), but this is deceiving. The more time we spend away from home, the more we notice the differences. This time away affects our reactions to our experiences, whether we look for a bigger meaning in small details or we downplay the significant differences that are obvious to others. Deciphering what is significant and what is not can be difficult.

So, although globalisation has shrunk the world, and technology enables us to communicate more quickly, this does not mean fewer differences, just more opportunities to make mistakes and learn. **So much information is available to anybody now that it gives people the illusion of being an expert in anything they google. Just because something is written and published recently, it does not mean it is true or up to date.**

Our brain is designed to discover new things when we travel, though locals would probably not notice. It is also constantly 'template matching', helping us make sense of our experience by triggering thoughts in our conscious mind (Wow, that's weird!) or provoking physiological responses (such as blushing); they are largely the result of mental conditioning we don't normally notice. The unconscious mind is like a gatekeeper to our conscious mind: it decides what to notice and what to ignore. The longer we stay in a new place, the more human interactions we have, the more powerful reactions (cognitive impact) we might experience. That's why it is important to understand how our minds work.

Why diversity and new environment are so tiring

Cultural background programs our thinking and behaviour in an unconscious way. That's the reason why, when we communicate across cultures, we often jump to the wrong conclusions, become offended, feel frustrated, or get the impression those people lack common sense. We might think our conscious mind is in control, but that is an illusion. Conscious and unconscious minds work separately, and both influence our behaviour. While we are fully aware of what is going on in the conscious mind, we have no idea of what information is stored in the unconscious mind.

The **intuitive (or unconscious) mind** draws on implicit knowledge, evaluates situations, makes judgements, and produces urges and intuition. The conscious mind draws on explicit knowledge. Experts have given these minds different names: for example, Daniel Kahneman, author of *Thinking, Fast and Slow*, calls them System 1 (fast-thinking, intuitive) and System 2 (slow-thinking, reflective, analytical). The two minds access different types of knowledge.

System 1 creates impressions and feelings that, when endorsed by System 2, become beliefs, attitudes, and intentions. In a foreign environment, we may see only what we expect to see. If the impression is strong, we can easily find things that confirm our biases. The intuitive mind relies on a predictable environment and generates automatic responses. We react automatically to particular stimuli. Foreign experiences force us to discover cultural patterns within our own mind. finding out that our sense of normal is rooted in our cultural configuration can be destabilising, because when two 'normals' collide, we start questioning everything we considered normal (or right). This can catch anyone off guard. **Common sense is based on what we consider right and what we believe to be true, values and beliefs we are not even aware of.**

The biggest culture gaps are within countries not between them

When we talk about managing across cultures, we tend to think of the words *culture* and *country* interchangeably. For example, it is a widely accepted notion that in Eastern countries, such as China and Japan, cultural norms dictate group harmony take precedence over individual recognition and achievement in the workplace. In Western countries, such as the USA and Germany, stronger emphasis is placed on individual accomplishment and performance at work. So, managers refer to 'Japanese culture' or the 'American way' of doing things when referencing work-related beliefs, norms, values, behaviours, and practices. The assumption country equals culture results in expat managers trying to do things the Japanese way in Japan, the Brazilian way in Brazil, and so on.

Bradley Kirkman, Vas Taras, and Piers Steel challenged this common understanding in a study published in *Management International Review* (*Harvard Business Review*, 2016). They used a research tool called 'meta-analysis' (essentially the study of studies) to analyse 558 existing studies, conducted over the last 35 years, on work-related values from 32 countries around the world, including the USA, Brazil, France, South Africa, and China. They concluded the following four work-related values addressed what people in all countries considered important:

1. Individuals vs. groups
2. Hierarchy and status in organisations
3. Having as much certainty as possible at work
4. Material wealth, assertiveness, and competition vs. societal welfare and harmony in relationships

Using these values, the team found that a country is actually a very poor 'container' of culture. They compared the extent of differences on the values *within* each country versus

58

the extent of differences *between* countries. If country were a good container of culture, we would expect fewer within-country differences (people in each country have similar shared values) and greater between-country differences (people in one country have different values from those in another).

Interestingly, they found the opposite. Specifically**, over 80% of the differences were found** *within* **countries and fewer than 20% of the differences** *between* **countries.** One of the reasons for this is decades of immigration across countries, leading to more diversity of values within each country.

If workplace cultures do not neatly cluster within national borders, what determines how they group together? To answer this question, they compared culture to 17 other possible containers, including personal characteristics (gender, age, generation, education level, occupation, and socio-economic status) and environment characteristics (civil and political freedom, economic freedom, GDP/capita, Human Development Index, Globalization Index, long-term unemployment, urbanisation, income inequality using the Gini coefficient, level of corruption, crime rate, and employment in agriculture). **Out of this list, country was the fifteenth best container of culture, or third worst with only gender and age cohorts ranking lower**. Interestingly a lot of new companies specialise in teaching clients about millennials and gender differences, the only two categories that are even less reliable than country.

The analysis showed demographic groupings such as occupation and socio-economic status were superior to country when capturing similarity in work-related values between people. What that means is, if we put a bunch of physicians from different countries together in a room, they are likely to have more shared work-related values compared to a group of random people from the same country. Likewise, people in similar socio-economic conditions or with similar levels of education would have more shared values among themselves than with groups from their birth country. And political and economic characteristics such as globalisation or economic freedom were all superior to country of origin for predicting similarity in work-related values. In other words, the data show it makes much more sense to talk about cultures of professions, rich versus poor, free versus oppressed, than about cultures of countries.

After all, some country borders were arbitrarily drawn based on political considerations and other historical events. Even though it's simple to refer to Russian or Malaysian or Argentinian culture, the diversity of values found within each of these countries makes this an extremely inexact and perhaps even dangerous practice when applied on an individual level.

For those who do business globally, the most important takeaway is never to assume people from a particular country embody the values typically associated with that country. Cultural stereotyping by country likely contributes to a whole host of mistakes when trying to lead and motivate a culturally diverse workforce. As noted earlier, courses offering advice on how to manage, say, Germans, are grossly misleading. Offering a course on how to manage people in Germany would be much more realistic.

Culture teaches us social norms, a set of rules we should live by if we want to be accepted by society. But is that how we really feel inside? Or, can we find our own culture frustrating? **Do we follow the rules because of tradition, fear, or choice?** We have seen and experienced a different way of life; why do we have to stick to our original culture's norms? How does this affect us when we travel, do business abroad, or meet other nationalities?

I read a very interesting blog by Chris Smit, a well-known cross-cultural trainer. He was discussing the question of culture vs. personality, which he stated was invalid. After reading Smit's argument, I found an example in the blog that is rather relevant to our discussion. Here is a fraction of it:

My personal experience is that culture plays a much larger role in everyday life than Hofstede's definition "allows". One day, I was having a meeting in Japan with a Japanese colleague. He told me very bluntly how he disliked his job and disliked his boss even more. This gave me the idea that he had a very direct personality. However, the next day, when we were having a meeting with a Japanese team, at which I was the only European, he blended in seamlessly with the rest of his colleagues. In the meeting, he displayed collectivistic behaviour.

I have seen this countless times. People in their own culture need to behave according to its rules in order to be accepted. But that does not necessarily mean it is how they feel or make decisions when outside the sphere of pressure placed upon them by their culture.

I have lived in the UK for over 15 years. And, when I go to Hungary to see my parents and family, I feel a bit lost sometimes. I kind of remember the little habits and traditions, the way of life there. But that is no longer me. I have experienced different cultures, and they have all shaped me. Today, more and more people live like that. They have their background and heritage, but they are now global citizens who are not constrained by their indigenous traditions and microculture.

When we grow up somewhere, we accept it as being the norm. It is what we know and adapt to. When we travel and live with other nationalities, we see more options. And, based on our experience and personality, we can adopt new ways of thinking and, sometimes, contradictory values. The world has changed; it is faster and smaller than ever. This does not mean that national cultures are not important or that they will disappear. It means a person's cultural orientation is not as obvious today as it was in the past. We don't necessarily know what influenced them. **Culture is what we are used to, not who we are. There can be a significant gap between what is natural to us and what is normal around us.** That kind of distinction can completely shift the way we experience the world around us.

This is where we can make a big mistake with training seminars. Preparing clients for a project that involves people of other nationalities can be as useful as it is dangerous. People tend to categorise information. If we think the Japanese colleague described earlier is going to be typically Japanese, our cognitive bias is going to kick in. Then, if he is the opposite of what we expect, we will try to alter the information to make it fit our preconceptions. When the Japanese colleague behaves as expected with his Japanese co-workers, but then behaves very differently away from them, his behaviour can confuse us even more.

This means two important things. One, to talk about Japanese or American or Brazilian culture leaves a lot of room for error. With such great differences among work-related values within each country, the notion we can generalise about a country's work culture is just plain wrong. And two, an American walking down the street in Shanghai is likely to meet many Chinese people with values closer to his or her own than to an 'average' Chinese. Assuming national cultural stereotypes apply to most individuals in a country simply does not work.

I have to emphasise something to avoid any misunderstanding. **I would never question the existence of statistically average national values and norms. My research is about understanding how they affect individual behaviour when a person's preferences are significantly different which is much more than we might realise.** For instance, people tend to be rather indirect in the UK. I am much more direct compared to them and know I have to adapt my communication style to make it more like theirs, or they might perceive me as rude or impolite. The UK 'normal' is not mine, and there is nothing wrong with that. It is my responsibility to notice the difference and make an effort. Dealing with people from other countries can be as difficult as interacting with individuals from other generations, departments, professions, or educational levels. All of those are just different cultural groups with their 'normal' and accepted way of acting, thinking, and communicating.

Stressful misunderstandings

The main source of stress and pain in life is the picture in our heads of how the world is supposed to be does not match the world outside. **Our perception is based on our values and is conditioned by the feedback and reaction of the people around us.** Once we understand this, we can change the rules. The more we understand how our minds work—the patterns, processes, values, and beliefs—the more we can bridge the disconnect within ourselves and between others.

When two people meet and interact, they run a test on each other. For example, if you and I meet, and I don't react or behave the way you expect or consider 'normal', you might feel disappointed or suspicious. We trust what is familiar and predictable to us. The thing is, I might feel the same about you. We judge others by their behaviour, we judge ourselves by our intentions, and we make assumptions about the other person's intentions that might be completely wrong. This is the basis of 80% of interpersonal issues, and it just gets more complicated across different cultural groups.

Once we understand the why behind behaviour, the quality of our relationship with ourselves and others dramatically improves. The WHY is our underlying set of values and beliefs. ICQ is not just about etiquette, but about the psychology of human behaviour and performance, the basis of personal development.

Luckily there are managers at work whose main responsibility is to bring out the best in their staff and support them. At least that's the theory.

Where strategy fails

Who are the unhappiest among our workers? And what's driving them crazy? They may not be who we think they are.

A study conducted by *Harvard Business Review* has revealed a shocking discovery that explains why employee engagement and diversity programs fail so dramatically despite the increasing amount of investment in them. It turns out the bottom 5% of the disengaged workforce, **the most disengaged employees, are middle managers,** the ones who could best be described as being "stuck in the middle".

Middle managers lead 80% of the workforce, and yet they get the least amount of support. The quality of their people and leadership skills directly affects employee engagement, performance, execution of strategies, and level of customer service. They gain their stereotypical reputation of being tyrants because they feel stressed and frustrated by not being able to handle these situations.

This is not an attack on middle management but the exact opposite. Traditionally the best employees are promoted to leadership roles, a completely new job, without any formal training. What if your boss told you that you got promoted to be a dentist and from tomorrow she/he would give you hassle because you are not a good dentist? It would not makes sense, yet, similar forces shape the corporate world. Being a good waiter does not necessarily translate into being a good restaurant manager. **Managing is a different job that requires actual training, not just the repetition of 'best practices' learned before the promotion which ultimately turns people into the kind of leader they never wanted to have.**

If a company has an employee engagement problem, it has a leadership problem. People leave managers, not companies. People aren't engaged by programs; they are engaged by people. It's that simple. We can no more manage the performance of people based on their annual review than we can manage our marriage based on how we celebrate our wedding anniversary.

So why aren't companies investing in transforming middle management?

The answer is they often don't know where to invest to be sure of a positive return. As a result, most companies resort to what they've used before and tweak it. But it won't make any difference. Most businesses spend less on training their managers than they do on the office furniture and PC they give them to work with. This is partly because often training doesn't deliver what's promised.

An analysis by Mind Gym identified seven core talents that matter most. Of these, one has a magnifying, or minimising, effect on all the rest. This is the ability to form, redefine, repair, maintain and, on occasion, exit from working relationships. The capability of understanding and leveraging personal and cultural differences is the competitive advantage of successful companies.

We can have the best strategy, the most expensive employee engagement and wellness program, but who is going to implement them? The most disengaged, forgotten layer of our company, the filter between senior management and employees. They have to manage up and down. They have the least amount of support but experience the most stress. How does that impact the business? What happens when a filter is clogged up? It blocks (and/or contaminates) the incoming and outgoing air, which leads to the breakdown of both the system and the people.

People think, behave, and work in such different ways it causes stress, confusion, and disengagement. This issue gets much worse across different cultural groups such as ethnicity, generation, gender, and profession, and managers need to deal with it. Managers are not just the key to productivity; they also unlock solutions to many business challenges. Their ability to work with the blueprint of individual and group mindset is crucial for the success of the company.

But how can they be experts in hundreds of different cultures, personality types, and their different combinations if they already have too much to do? Should they focus on culture or personality?

CHAPTER **5**

The Connection Between Personality and Culture

"One of the greatest regrets in life is being what others would want you to be, rather than being yourself."
– Shannon L. Alder

Here is the question. What's more important: personality or cultural background? Countless frameworks exist for both. Not surprisingly, a lot of coaches and trainers are certified in one and the other because they instinctively feel there is a connection. That connection is even stronger and more logical than they think.

Personality is a tricky concept. It is often based on the childhood experiences that formed the story of who we are. At the same time, we keep making choices that support our own narrative. The idea of personality can trap us in a safe and familiar pattern of being, even if we don't really like it. Most of our personality is shaped by fear—of embarrassment, or of losing face, or of being unpopular, for example. According to other theories, it is influenced by the most efficient strategies we have developed to gain the love of the person whose attention we used to crave the most as children.

To boil it down, personality is a history of our habits, a collection of best practices that meet our needs and reflect our values.

Often we define ourselves so much by our environment we have no idea who we are without it. At other times, we tend to be so loyal to the idea of our personality, we never find out who we could be. We say no to new opportunities and avoid challenges, so we don't feel miserable or uncomfortable. **Unfortunately, the result of avoidance isn't safety and security but lower self-esteem and loss of self-respect, which ultimately endanger everything we are so desperate to protect.** Understanding how these processes work can give us the feeling of more control and less stress.

We use mental models to represent how things work. Our brain forms them automatically by noticing patterns in what we experience each day. Very often, however, those models are not completely accurate. Education can make them more precise by enabling us to internalise the knowledge and experiences other people have collected throughout their lives. Then, by correcting and updating our models, we can begin to think about what we are doing more clearly, which helps us make better decisions, too.

Self-awareness is a superpower. Although it is freely available to anyone, not many people are willing to pay the price for it. Once we take responsibility for our own development, we are in a very different league. Whatever our inner demons, we are already ahead of others who, by refusing to face their own, choose to waste their potential. What's more, this evasiveness often negatively impacts the people around them.

When I was a kid my father seldom encouraged me to try something new. For some reason, he always had a problem with every opportunity. Don't do martial arts, you'll get hurt. Don't go to university in the capital, you'll get lost. Don't move abroad, you won't succeed. Don't buy a car, you'll spend too much money maintaining it.

I still carry some of that burden with me, and to this day I have never owned a car. (On the other hand, he was right about a few things.) But once I identified the problem, and how it started, I was able to change it instead of blaming my father or feeling frustrated. That was my responsibility.

The binary choice: pain or pleasure

Let's deep dive into our souls and find out why we do what we do exactly. Although the human mind is very complex, its guiding principles are not. Once we have a clear picture of how the human mind works, it is easy to find better ways to get things done and work more effectively with others.

Businesses are built *by* people *for* people, so the more we understand our employees and clients, the more successful our businesses can become. According to *Harvard Business Review*, the number one criterion for advancement and promotion for professionals is an **ability to communicate effectively.**

If we really want to be effective, we need to understand the pain–pleasure principle when interacting with other people. Everyone talks, everyone communicates, but only very few connect. Every single day, a fierce battle is being waged for our attention as we are bombarded with over 35,000 messages. Which ones do we notice? Who do we listen to and why? The answer is less obvious than we would assume.

People are complex but predictably different. Every decision we make is dependent on our values and needs. We make decisions that lean towards things we deem positive and perceive as pleasurable. We also make decisions that move us away from things we've determined are not as gratifying. The pleasure-pain principle was originated by Sigmund Freud in modern psychoanalysis, although Aristotle noted the significance in his 'Rhetoric', more than 300 years BC.

This decision is subconscious, but what we consider painful or pleasurable is subjective. For example, training in the gym might be pleasurable for you and painful for me. The point is, the way I interpret going to the gym is going to determine what I do about it: I get excited and join you, or I find an excuse and watch TV. The challenge is most of us are unaware of what triggers our response.

We might recognise the patterns (habits) and try to change the behaviour; however, it is unlikely to be successful or sustainable if we do not replace the unresourceful behaviour with a resourceful one. Do we know how we can change those psychological needs?

We can't.

But we can change the behaviour that satisfies those needs if we know why we are behaving in a certain way.

Some basic rules about pain and pleasure exist, and I encourage you to reflect on them, find personal examples in your life, and spot the process you go through. Once you do that, you have the power to change if you want to. It's your responsibility to develop the ability to choose your response.

Rule #1: All decisions made by human beings are to avoid pain or gain pleasure

When it comes to motivation and why people do the things they do, it's down to the basic science of pain versus pleasure. In its simplest form, all decisions human beings make are either to gain pleasure or to avoid pain. Any act can be broken down this way. Why do we brush our teeth? Why would a woman spend precious time applying makeup before going out? All these actions can be reduced to an individual trying to attain pleasure and/or avoid the pain that an action is going to bring.

Rule #2: People do much more to avoid pain than to gain pleasure

As it turns out, while human beings want to avoid pain and gain pleasure, they do more for one than the other. Avoiding immediate pain is much more motivating than gaining immediate pleasure. If a tiger were chasing you, and you spotted a suitcase full of money on the ground, it's unlikely you would stop to pick it up. Studies have demonstrated time and time again people do much more to avoid short-term pain than to gain short-term pleasure. Loss aversion is one of the strongest forces shaping our decisions.

Rule #3: Perception IS reality!

It's the perception of pain and pleasure, not actual pain and pleasure, that drives people. At first, this concept might seem a bit strange, but in fact it's rather obvious. Because we can't ever know for sure what the future holds, our brain, and specifically the prefrontal cortex within the frontal lobe, is constantly making assumptions and judgements about the future based on our past experience. It's this perception of future pain and pleasure that drives our actions. Unfortunately, it turns out our perceptions are often very flawed, especially when it comes to things that are a bit more complex than running away from a predator or falling from a height.

Our greatest advantage is often the biggest disadvantage that holds us back: the modern brain and in particular the neocortex. It allows us to be logical and objective while giving us the unique ability to create vivid memories and imagine unlimited future scenarios. As a matter of fact, there is an overlap between facts and invention. We tend to believe our memories are accurate although it is likely that nearly 50% of them are heavily reconstructed based on what have experienced since then, what meaning we attached to those events and how we

71

subconsciously kept them consistent with our other storylines. This process can be used to predict the future, as well.

Here's an example. A zebra gets really stressed when a predator chases it, but if it makes it out alive, its stress level goes back to normal and Stripy is back to grazing. It does not think about it twenty times a day, nor does it go around telling all the other zebras about the event while making it sound even more heroic than it was. But when something happens to us humans, we find it much more difficult to let it go. By repeating the story in our heads, and throwing in some assumptions, and then adding in some exciting detail, we prevent our stress level from going down.

Reinterpreting the incident means being in a chronic state of stress. And that stress has exploded to an invisible $1 trillion health epidemic according to Peter Schnall's book, *Unhealthy Work*. That's more than the cost of cancer, diabetes, and heart disease combined. Stress is a factor in five out of the six leading causes of death: heart disease, cancer, stroke, lower respiratory disease, and accidents. An estimated 75–90% of all doctor visits are for stress-related issues (The American Institute of Stress).

Most of the time the root cause of the stress is in our mindset, so wouldn't it make sense to learn how to use it? I really wish mindset were taught in schools.

Rule #4: Pain and pleasure are modulated by time

Not only are we trying to avoid what we perceive to be painful and attain what we perceive to be pleasurable, but timing also matters. We focus on avoiding immediate pain and trying to attain immediate pleasure. The closer something is to this moment, the more pain or pleasure we attach to it. Therefore, pain tomorrow is not as powerful a force as pain today. Pain in a decade is absolutely less motivating (or more demotivating) than pain a week from now. This is precisely why most of us have such a hard time saving money even though it means we receive interest (free money) by delaying spending.

As time goes on, our perception of pain and pleasure changes. Every decision we make results in at least one or more of the following: short-term pain, long-term pain, short-term pleasure, or long-term pleasure. Short term always wins over long term unless there is a substantial amount of pain or pleasure associated with the long-term avoidance of pain or gain of pleasure.

For example, being stressed or tired prompts our craving for instant gratification, which explains the lack of will power at the end of the day. Once I asked a group of senior leaders if they found it difficult to change their behaviour and stick to a new routine. The honest and clear answer was "Yes, every Monday!"

Rule #5: Emotion trumps logic when thinking of pain and pleasure

There is also a strong emotional aspect to making a decision based on gaining pleasure or avoiding pain. How many times have you looked longingly at a dish of ice cream and then gone ahead and eaten it even though you knew it wasn't the healthiest choice? We've all been there. Logically, you know you shouldn't have the ice cream, but you *want* the ice cream. What wins? Intellect or emotion?

An ounce of emotion wins over an ounce or two of logic every time. The pain or pleasure related to our emotions is hardwired in our brains to be much stronger, because it's the primitive part of our brain that tells us to act rather than think ahead. This also further explains the modulation of pain and pleasure by time. When something is going to happen now, it's much more likely to trigger an emotional response in us than something that is going to happen decades from now.

Rule #6: Survival vs. desire in the pleasure and pain principle

Finally, any time our survival response is triggered, everything else essentially shuts down because pain and pleasure can be further broken down into things that are hardwired for survival and things that are mere wants. It's easy, then, to understand that if something sets off a survival response, such as running away from a predator, that response is going to override just about every other desire in the moment.

Wanting to consume sugar or other addictive foods is the perfect example of something that is hardwired. If you love cookies and someone puts one in front of you, you are instinctually driven to eat it. Now, many times we can use enough logic and future pain to stop ourselves, but over 50% of the US (and other) population loses that battle several times per day! We are hardwired to eat sugar to stay alive, and while processed foods are only a hundred years old, our genetics are more than a hundred thousand years old! From a survival perspective, the more calories, the better. Our brain thinks eating the cookie means survival and not eating it means death. It even sounds logical. Human biology is optimised for conditions that existed all those thousands of years ago, not for the world we actually live in. We are all running a demanding new software on ancient hardware.

What we consider pain or pleasure depends on what we need, value, and are scared of. What we need and want becomes our pleasure, and the opposite becomes the pain we want to avoid.

Here's the bad news. Every single day we have around 60,000-90,000 thoughts, and 90% of those are pretty much the same as the day before. Around 70% of those are negative (Joe Dispenza, 2014). That is how our brain works. It is designed to spot danger to keep us alive, which is why we tend to come up

74

with negative assumptions about situations. How many times have you heard gossip that painted a positive picture about the person being talked about? My guess (and experience) is it could not have been too many.

Our body is not much different. What percentage of our body can feel mild to extreme pain? Nearly 100%. What percentage of our body can feel mild to extreme pleasure if the circumstances are ideal? That's much more limited, isn't it?

A limited number of levers beneath the surface

There are six basic, universal needs that make humans tick and drive all our behaviour. Combined, they are the force behind the crazy things (other) people do and the great things we do. According to Tony Robbins (American author, philanthropist, and life coach) we all have the same six needs, but how we value those needs and in what order determines the direction of our lives. We are all a combination of the four personality types governed by the six human needs and shaped by our environment.

Need 1: Certainty/Comfort

The first human need is the need for certainty. It's our need to feel in control and to know what's coming next so we can feel secure. It's the need for basic comfort, for avoiding pain and stress, and for creating pleasure. Our need for certainty is a survival mechanism. It affects how much risk we're willing to take in life—in our jobs, in our investments, in our relationships. The higher the need for certainty, the less risk we're willing to take or emotionally bear. By the way, this is where real 'risk tolerance' comes from.

Need 2: Uncertainty/Variety

Let me ask you a question: Do you like surprises? If you answered yes, you're kidding yourself! We like the surprises we want. The ones we don't, we call problems. But we still need them to put some muscle in our lives. We can't grow muscle, or character, unless we have something to push against.

Need 3: Significance

We all need to feel important, special, unique, or needed. So how do we achieve significance? Sometimes through earning billions of dollars or collecting academic degrees—distinguishing ourselves with a master's degree or a PhD. We can build a giant Twitter following. Or we put tattoos and piercings all over ourselves, even in places we don't talk about. We can also achieve significance by having more or bigger problems than anybody else. "You think *your* husband's bad? Take mine for a day!" Of course, we can get there by being more spiritual (or pretending to be).

Spending a lot of money can make us feel significant, and so can spending very little. We all know people who constantly brag about their bargains or who feel special because they heat their homes with cow manure and sunlight. Some very wealthy people gain significance by hiding their wealth.

Need 4: Connection/Love

The fourth basic need is connection. It is the oxygen of life; it's what we all want and need most. We can get a sense of connection through intimacy, or friendship, or prayer, or walking in nature. If nothing else works, we can get a cat (highly recommended: we have two).

These first four needs are what we call the needs of the personality. We all find ways to meet them—by working harder, or coming up with a big problem, or creating stories to rationalise them.

The last two are the needs of the spirit. These are rarer. Not all of us meet them, but when we do, we truly feel fulfilled.

Need 5: Growth

If a relationship is not growing, if a business is not growing, if we are not growing, it doesn't matter how much money we have in the bank, how many friends we have, how many people love us—we are not going to experience real fulfilment. And the reason we grow, I believe, is so we have something of value to give.

Need 6: Contribution

Corny as it may sound, the secret to living is giving. Life's not about me but about us. Think about it. What's the first thing we do when we get good or exciting news? We call somebody we love and share it with them. Sharing enhances everything we experience.

These psychological needs are not absolute, which might seem like a contradiction. Do we need variety and certainty at the same time? Technically yes. What matters is the proportion. Imagine certainty and variety as a sliding scale, or as though you were standing on a seesaw trying to find your balance. We are somewhere in between the two extremes. Some people need more variety, some much more certainty. Life is a dynamic process, but our brain loves homeostasis—it does not like big changes. Our preference on the certainty–variety scale is like a thermostat. If we experience too much variety in our lives, we crave more certainty. **We can get to the point where we need at least the illusion of certainty and familiarity so much that we are willing to tell and accept lies about the past and future instead of facing the truth in the present moment where we can actually do something.** On the other hand, if we have too much certainty for our liking, we get bored and will likely create some exciting or challenging situations.

The same principle applies to significance and belonging. We want to feel important, but we also want to be part of the group. Where's your sweet spot? Some people love being in the spotlight, others prefer to feel harmony and stability. One is not better than the other.

Unfortunately, most of us are unaware of our own preferences. We chase a feeling without really knowing why. Let's assume five people have the same need for certainty. How do they satisfy that need? One might have a strict morning routine; another might be a micromanager; the third loves eating and drinking; the fourth plans every step of the day; the fifth constantly asks questions to clarify what someone else is saying. All seemingly different activities, and each person might criticise the other for their particular behaviour, never realising it all stems from the same psychological need, certainty.

Our personality is a portfolio of best practices we learned to meet our needs and reflect our values. Our behaviour is the visible part of our identity which is often a different set of best practices depending on the circumstances.

The table below lays out examples of good and bad behaviours that can meet the same needs.

Core Needs	Resourceful Behaviours	Un-resourceful Behaviours
Certainty	Cleaning, foundation routine, rituals, organisation, Backing self, certainty of self, allowing yourself who you need to become in order to handle the problem.	Over eating, Control of others, watching hours of TV instead of having a life, rut, obsessive compulsive behaviour, procrastination.
Uncertainty / Variety	New challenges, playfulness, embracing adventure, changing the meaning of an event (reframe), different hobbies, creativity.	Overwhelm, drug taking, intoxication, changing TV channels, self sabotage, creating drama and problems for ourselves so we have 'something to do'.
Significance	Leader of self and others, volunteer work, speaking up, achieving a goal, mastery in our field of endeavour.	Putting others down, promiscuity, gossip, sad stories about self, martyr, victim, lying in a way that gets us caught, rebellion
Connection/Love	Sharing, supporting others, connect through nature, faith, self love, self worth, your truth, unconditional love, interdependent relationships	Needy, self harm, unhealthy relationships, connection through problem e.g drugs, 'if you don't love me I'll hurt myself'
Growth	Lifelong learning, pursuit of mastery, learning to teach	Information gathering without applying
Contribution	Paying it forward, donating to charity, volunteering, helping people, doing things for others.	Being a Martyr, giving without learning to take care of self, giving to get.

The 6 human needs by Tony Robbins

Here's a wild thought, and please let me know what you think about it. This is my take on values: ***The ways we consider right to meet our needs are our values.***

How to pick up chicks

We all have a set of personal values that dictate how we interact with and judge other people. Our values also determine how we view ourselves and how we see the world. We have pet peeves and a perceived concept of how things 'should' be.

If somebody does not talk to us in terms of our values, the message is likely to fall on deaf ears. Cultural intelligence (ICQ) does not mean we try to please everyone and deny ourselves. It is about finding the balance. What do I mean exactly?

There are three types of communication according to Dr. John F. Demartini (professional speaker, author, business consultant):

Careless: We project our own values and we want to change others.

Careful: We speak in terms of other people's values, which is like walking on eggshells.

Both options are guaranteed to fail in the long run. We get upset with each other all the time because someone did something to violate some personal 'value' of ours. In unhealthy relationships, each person uses the other as a constant sounding board for some rule the other one has violated. And while sometimes our rules are valid, at other times they are just plain silly. We often impose our values on our partner without telling them about our expectations or needs, which only results in disappointment and frustration.

Caring: We talk about something important to us in terms of the values the other person has. Here's an example. A 19-year-old kid's mum was complaining he wasn't doing very well at school, so she asked Dr Demartini to help who quickly got into the conversation:

- So what is important to you? What do you really want?
- I like picking up 'chicks'.
- Interesting. What do you think those 'chicks' want?
- They like successful and rich men.
- I see. How can you have money and success?
- I need a good job in a big company.
- Right. How do you get that?
- I need good grades so I can get a degree.
- And how do you get good grades?
- I have to study.
- So the more you study, the more women will like you?
- Oh…

This is how quickly everything changed. The point is to link a goal to his values, in this case, picking up chicks. He had to realise doing well at school was going to make him more successful and respected, which was ultimately going to get him some love. When his mum talked to him in terms of her own values (stable job, good grades), he did not listen. When somebody else spoke his language, he did. When we care about someone, we understand what they value, and we speak in their terms. **In a business situation, caring is called *selling* or *leading*.**

How would you ask your dad, mum, or brother to borrow their car? Would you say the same thing the same way to make that happen? Kids can be really good at changing the way they deliver a message depending on who they are talking to. When I was a child, I knew my mum really wanted to look after me, so I had to be slightly needy to get some pocket money from her. When I went to my father for money, I had to make sure whatever I needed it for cost much more than what I was asking. So, the option of forking out some money was a bargain for my father and a long-term investment in my future (and therefore in his, too).

The real question is: Where do these rules come from? Do we just make them up as we go along?

What are your personal values?

Personal values are the feelings and sentiments we hold about ourselves and the world around us. These feelings become so deeply ingrained in us we forget they only apply to our lives and not to the world in general. We often adopt our beliefs and values as we grow up. Ever hear the phrase, "You are the average of the five people you spend the most time with"? We pick up little pieces from other people, our family, friends, and significant others—or at least the characteristics we like. Then we discard the ones we don't. The end result is our existing values and beliefs. Both help us determine whether something is 'good' or 'bad.' **Values are what we consider right, beliefs are what we believe to be true.**

As we turn to our personal values as a source of guidance throughout our lives, they begin to make a lasting impact. Our rules shape us and make us who we are. There's nothing wrong with that! It's when our rules become unreasonable and make our relationships more difficult that we need to re-evaluate and reshape our beliefs and values, so they create harmony, not conflict. When there's a clash between two people's common sense, we experience personal and cultural differences. **That is what cultural differences are: clashes of common sense.**

The challenge with all these beliefs and values is they can limit future decisions about who we are and what we are capable of. We need to remember most of our beliefs are generalisations about our past, based on our interpretations of painful and pleasurable experiences.

Again, the challenge is threefold:

1. Most of us do not consciously decide what we are going to believe.

2. Often our beliefs are based on misinterpretation of past experiences.

3. Once we adopt a belief, we forget it is merely an interpretation. We begin to treat our beliefs as if they

81

were realities. In fact, we rarely, if ever, question our long-held beliefs. If you ever wonder why people do what they do, remember human beings do not act randomly. All our actions are the result of our beliefs. Those beliefs have different levels of emotional certainty and intensity, and it's important to know just how intense they are.

It is vital to be aware of our own hierarchy of values because they determine how we see others and how others see us. Everything is relative.

Let's take a personal example. My most important values are integrity, family, work. If I promise to do something for you, I'm going to get it done. But if I get a phone call telling me a family member has had an accident and is in hospital, I'm going to break my promise, at least temporarily, because family is higher up on my value chain than work.

Comparing apple and pear?

Let's make it even more personal and talk about my favourite topic, myself. Technically that is not true, however most people love talking about themselves.

What if I need more significance in my life than belonging? What if I need more variety than certainty? What if I believe in individualism rather than collectivism, or if competition drives me more than co-operation? What if I think short term, not long term? Would I behave similarly to someone with opposing preferences? No. Extroverted people who want to be in charge and have the need to win are going to behave differently from those who are more introverted, who need harmony and belonging because they dislike challenges and confrontation. **We behave in a way that reflects our values and supports our needs. That is the key.**

I am aware I have just contradicted something I said a few chapters earlier: **our personality determines how we want to behave, and culture determines how we should behave.** It seems like a paradox, just like our psychological needs and values, but it is not. There is a balance. **My values and needs determine how I want to behave, unless my environment forces me to pretend to be someone else by conforming to the norms.**

When we join a new group (company, club, etc.), we are not sure what to do so we tend to look around and copy the behaviour around us. We check out what is 'normal', what is acceptable, and what is frowned upon. Later on, we loosen up a bit and show more of ourselves. Unless we get really stressed, our true personality is not likely to bust through the thick layer of social conformity for a while.

Culture is what we are used to, not who we are, but it is not always obvious. How many people have you met (it might even be you) who felt uncomfortable in their environment, who felt like outsiders because everyone else seemed so similar? Was something wrong with the rest of them? No, individually they probably felt the same internal friction, but they also bought into the accepted and encouraged behavioural style (cultural norms) around them.

Like individual behaviour, **culture is a group habit driven by values and needs**. A lot of experts claim it is impossible and wrong to compare personality, behaviour and culture. I think it would be a crime not to because the underlying forces are the same: a group of people with similar needs and values get together to make life easier for themselves; they accept certain behaviours, habits, and communication styles as normal; naturally they trust and like each other as they are very similar.

People who grow up in the USA are used to a particular lifestyle: time is money, competition is fierce, achievement is more important than a title, success comes before quality of life, etc. Does it mean those are their own needs and values? If that were true, life would be much easier for them.

If the gap between who we are inside and who we pretend to be is too wide, it drains us, requiring too much energy from us and leading to burn out, stress, or even worse. If we top that up with the feeling of not being good enough, of not being normal, of being an outsider or a fraud, it can lead to serious health issues. The more stress we experience, the more we revert to our natural style and the more it highlights the gap we feel should not be seen by others. That's one vicious cycle. So, how do we get out of it? Do we have to?

This dilemma is why ICQ is vital. Once we understand the concept, we will know ourselves and begin to realise nothing is wrong with us. We each have different strengths and weaknesses, and that is perfectly fine. Instead of trying to be 'normal', or shall we say 'average', at other things, we should amplify our strengths and find complementary partners. That is how we create a high-performing team and find fulfilment.

Have you ever worked for someone and felt passionate about their work? It is very likely the team was led by someone who understood ICQ. Some people are naturals at this, but most of us need to learn it. It's an area where common sense and good intention can backfire, because trust, pain, pleasure, motivation, and respect are subjective. The way you gain my trust can be rather different from what I have to do to gain yours.

This is where a new breed of leaders excels and what intelligent global leadership is all about.

CHAPTER 6

Evolve or Dissolve

"Most people never run far enough on the first wind to find out they've got a second. Give your dreams all you've got, and you'll be amazed at the energy that comes out of you."

—William James

Building a business is about building relationships with people. Globalisation has shrunk the world, sped up communication, and toughened the competition for everyone. The only strategic advantage left is people, and the way we lead and serve them determines our success. It requires constant learning, and applying the latest solutions, or somebody else takes over. We must evolve or we are going to dissolve.

A new breed of global leaders

Intelligent Global Leaders are able to create synergy and trust in a diverse team by leveraging its personal and cultural differences. These leaders have **the mindset of an entrepreneur, the drive of an immigrant, and the charisma of a visionary**. They can bring together people who have a common future as opposed to no more than a common past, and they thrive in many environments where others are struggling.

We can try to ignore evolution, but we cannot deny it. As Charles Darwin said, "It is not the strongest of the species that survives but the one most adaptable to change."

What does it take to be an Intelligent Global Leader, and how is ICQ mindset a factor? Let's break it down.

ICQ, as noted throughout the book, stands for cultural intelligence, and in particular the ability to break down barriers within and between people. It requires understanding the blueprint of why people think and behave differently depending on their personality type *and* cultural background. CQ, on the other hand, primarily refers to country-specific approaches; it is also Dr David Livermore's trademark and the name of his excellent framework.

ICQ mindset refers to being able to see a situation from completely different perspectives, so we can make better decisions and connect the dots others do not notice. It involves the ability and will to find innovative solutions instead of protecting our egos and forcing our opinion onto others. It is the ability to choose to respond instead of just reacting.

Entrepreneurial mindset is a part of the ICQ mindset. Being an entrepreneur is considered cool nowadays. It's trendy. But I remember that in Hungary, where I grew up, it had a very different meaning, perhaps because of the communist legacy there. When somebody claimed to be an entrepreneur, it was almost as if they were saying, "What I do is none of your business. I'm not going to share any details with you because I don't trust you." The people who were listening simply assumed the 'entrepreneur' was doing something dodgy.

By contrast, Darren Hardy, author of *The Entrepreneur Roller Coaster*, would say an entrepreneur is a freak. If you look at his definition, you'll see this is a compliment: "A person who is obsessed with or unusually enthusiastic about a specific interest."

Entrepreneurs, too, are obsessed with their mission, living and breathing it, aware anything less won't work in a VUCA world. VUCA is an acronym used by the American Military to describe the extreme conditions in Afghanistan and Iraq. It stands for Volatile, Uncertain, Complex and Ambiguous. This terminology resonates with an increasing number of CEOs trying to make sense of the constantly changing challenges brought on by politics, economics, society, and the environment. Not many situations are more VUCA than managing people and global businesses.

Entrepreneurs are a special type of breed that thrives in this environment.

One reason for this is they have an **immigrant mentality.** When most immigrants leave their country, they give up everything they know to start a life in a new country where they have to perform and compete with people in a language that isn't their own. That's pretty hard. **Immigrants are happy with what they have but never satisfied, and that is a powerful combination.** As Gary Vaynerchuk has said several times on his podcast, *The Gary Vee Audio Experience*, "I wish everybody was an immigrant. It is a huge advantage."

In business, especially, the focus is on the value we provide. It doesn't matter where we are from.

I came to the UK 15 years ago and built a global business in a language that is not my mother tongue. It was not easy, but I believe I had an advantage. Instead of looking for excuses why I could not succeed, I focused on how to serve more people and add more value to their lives.

I am very grateful for every little thing while knowing I can achieve more. The way to do that is through discipline. Jocko Willink, the Navy SEAL turned author and leadership trainer, coined the term "discipline equals freedom". Discipline does not mean we say no to everything or that we have to be rigid. Inflexibility is dangerous, because it can break us.

The intellectual hamster syndrome

People are fascinated by mindset for a reason. Ever since I can remember, I have always wanted to find ways to upgrade myself. My plan wasn't too ambitious: I just no longer wanted to be an obese kid who was also doing well at the school where his mum was a teacher. (Not the best combination for a teenager who wanted to be accepted and maybe even a bit popular.) I kept reading and learning, but I could not really put all the theories I read about into practice. I was like an 'intellectual hamster'.

Have you ever watched hamsters eating? They fill up their face so much, they cannot even chew or swallow. Greedy little things. I did the same with books. I read so much I could not remember 99% of the content. Instead of practicing a key principle I had just learned, I went on to the next one.

I know a lot of people with a similar attitude. In the end, they tend to conclude the concepts they're studying don't work. Of course, they don't, unless we stop to practise them. We can hire a personal trainer, but he cannot do the push-ups for us.

So that was **phase one** of my personal development plan: the desperate attempt to stop feeling frustrated by the immense gap between my intention and results. I had some knowledge but no skills. I focused on tuition, not intuition. My rather self-centred goal was to minimise my embarrassment and potentially increase my chances of success.

Phase two began when I started working in a team. It is almost given employees don't get along at work, or they are not big fans of their bosses, but one of my most shocking experiences happened at the University of Sussex. My class was an exceptional one, full of very smart students. Most of them were between the ages of 25 and 35 with years of real-life skills and the drive to make their busy lives even busier by working full-time towards their MSc degree at the Science Policy Research Unit, ranked best in the world for development studies by QS World University Rankings 2017.

Sixteen people were assigned to work together, and the result was an intellectual blood bath. The mess brought up all kinds of memories from kindergarten: the facial expressions, the illogical and emotional outbursts, the power trips to prove who was smarter, the vying for leadership positioning (which, according to some collective PC decision made at the beginning, officially did not exist). I am pretty sure everyone has been part of something similar, and it makes you wonder how the people involved got a job at all.

Reading a case study can be interesting, but being a part of it costs a lot in terms of productivity, stress, and time and resources. That cost becomes much more pressing than the original challenge.

The Interaction Gap research discussed in Chapter 2 is not just a theory but is happening to all of us right now. Maybe we don't realise it's happening, or maybe we believe it's supposed to be like that, but this gap endangers our success both as leaders and as a part of a team. There is so much potential in a team, yet we cannot tap into it as much as we should be able to.

That's how I got started on **phase three**. I asked myself how I could help others level up their mindset so they could bring out the best in themselves and the rest of the team. There are many models and gurus out there, but who are the practitioners who make things happen? What do they have in common? What's stopping the intellectual hamsters from actually chewing and swallowing all the goodness in their mouth?

Taking souls, changing paradigms, and awakening giants

It is not about the number of techniques we have, but the intensity and mastery of those techniques that count. Remember the padded man experiment in Chapter 2? The more we practice a limited number of techniques, the more instinctive those techniques become.

One big powerful idea can change a person in an instant while the most scientifically validated book or framework cannot. When I got certified in different intercultural, leadership, coaching, and psychometric models, my assumption was there must be a huge overlap among those approaches. I figured they might use different definitions or colour charts, but there would be a common structure beneath the surface. We are all unique but predictably different so there can be only a limited number of levers. What are those? **Diversity is insanely complex on the surface, but it is simpler deep inside, where there are only a limited number of levers**. Why? There are a limited number of values and psychological needs people can have, but the way they meet those needs and reflect those values depending on how they prioritise them can be almost unlimited. Before we move on to the result of that research, let me show you what I mean.

Talking about mindset nowadays is more popular than ever. The topic of personal development used to be considered some new-age, voodoo, law-of-attraction scam, or a desperate attempt to get things right when people screwed up too often but were not yet ready to go to church. All that has changed. More and more inspiring stories are coming out and proving the power of our minds. Everybody has their favourite angle, but the more we delve into this subject, the more we realise the same topics are being discussed. It's the packaging that differs depending on what resonates with a particular audience.

Quantum physics, neuroscience, positive thinking, neuro-linguistic programming (NLP), mindfulness—all have much more in common than most people realise. **All are different paths to the same destination**. Let's take a look at some examples:

David Goggins is the toughest man in the world, an ex-Navy SEAL who transformed himself into one of America's fittest athletes through self-discipline, mental toughness, and hard work. His book, *Can't Hurt Me: Master Your Mind and Defy the Odds*, is like a detailed journal of both his life and his way of thinking. Goggins recognises people who feel stuck need more than an inspiring story.

They need both an example to look up to and a step-by-step guide showing them how to get there. One without the other one is less likely to work. Goggins is a practitioner, a leader who has gained control over his mindset and achieved world records that seemed impossible. He is a big fan of "callousing the mind", meaning "embracing the suck"—the daily grind of pushing through activities we do not feel like doing.

Bob Proctor, one of the most famous personal development gurus, specialises in shifting paradigms. It is his way of explaining how the mind works. A paradigm is a "multitude of habits that are lodged in the subconscious mind." These control over 95% of our actions and, if not aligned with what we consciously want to do, make it very likely we are going to do what we normally do. That is why change is difficult.

Luckily James Clear offers us a path to changing habits in his book, *Atomic Habits*. Clear hasn't come up with anything new but has successfully presented the information within a simple and understandable framework, peppered it with some uplifting stories, and sweetened it with scientific research to please a wider audience.

Joe Dispenza creates a bridge between true human potential and the latest scientific theories of neuroplasticity. He explains how thinking in new ways, as well as changing what we believe, can rewire our brain. He shows us the science proving that personality creates our personal reality, and that our personality is made up of how we think, how we act, and how we feel.

There are countless more authors who have gone through challenging situations and share their way of overcoming those obstacles. When their conviction and example create the kind of certainty that trumps doubt or pessimism, an audience starts paying attention and following them. These practitioners have a few things in common.

- They are real-life personalities who **became famous by facing their own demons**. They are living examples of their message.
- They do not try to solve every single problem in the world, and they do not claim their approach can fix everything. **They are clear about their mission**.
- **They have simplified their methods**, making them as uncomplicated as possible so others can use them. They are not trying to please people who love questioning everything and refuse to accept a solution that works if it is not scientifically validated (yet).
- **They connect dots others have not noticed.** They push their own boundaries and the limitations of their own fields. They have gone against norms because they realised the world has changed, what worked in the past might not work today, and questioning the status quo is not a sign of disrespect but a moral obligation.

All have made a difference in the lives of millions of people because they achieved uncommon things in unusual times. The underlying concepts are the same: developing their self-awareness, understanding their own drivers, and believing in the basic principles of how mindset works.

My own failures motivated me to follow those guidelines and crack the code of why people think and behave differently so they can level up their mindset and bring out the best in themselves and others.

Have I achieved that? Not yet. It is a never-ending quest, and I cannot imagine a more rewarding one. This book is not meant to be a silver bullet for every problem. I think of it more as a professional journal of insights, questions, stories, ideas, and a request for more research and collaboration instead of competition.

In the upcoming chapters, I am going share how I addressed the challenges discussed so far and the solutions my research produced.

CHAPTER 7

Thousands of Years of Research, Same Result

"Every man has three characters: that which he shows, that which he has, and that which he thinks he has."

– Alphonse Karr

Even though people are infinitely diverse in terms of their experiences and beliefs, everyone, regardless of age, race, culture, or gender, shares similar behavioural characteristics. One person you meet might be talkative, sociable, and loud, and another quiet, shy, and methodical. Some people like structure, some don't. Some like to move at a fast pace, others prefer to take their time.

Organisations that rely on teams to accomplish business goals can't afford to have personal differences get in the way of performance. They need to ensure team members are functioning in high-trust, low-friction environments. As part of creating high-performance workplaces, managers need to know which team members are best suited to certain types of work; salespeople need to create rapport with different types of prospects; recruiters need to understand a candidate's potential strengths and weaknesses; customer service reps need to communicate clearly. In virtually every profession and for every type of role on the planet, the ability to effectively deal with others significantly distinguishes star performers from average or poor performers.

The good news is researchers have discovered there are **four basic patterns of behaviour** that are both identifiable and predictable. Often referred to as an individual's **behavioural style**, these patterns are a person's natural way of doing things, the manner in which they tend to interact and communicate.

Understanding a behavioural model is the first step towards becoming a more effective communicator, because it explains a person's basic communication tendencies.

Effective communication involves the right combination of tone, words, body language, pace of speech, and actions—all of which are components of behavioural style. By understanding the common behavioural styles that exist, we can learn how to treat people in a way that allows them to feel comfortable with us so there will be less tension and better communication. This leads to increased trust, cooperation, respect, commitment, and productivity.

The classic era

The pre-Socratic philosopher **Empedocles** (c. 492–c. 432 BCE) was the first to use a four-factor model. Fifty years later, **Hippocrates** (c. 460–c. 370 BCE), the famous Greek physician and father of the Hippocratic Oath, further defined the four personality temperaments or *humours.* Each had its share of positive and negative traits, which could either benefit or hinder someone in professional or personal situations. It was rare for a person to fit solely within one of the temperaments. While any given temperament could be dominant, most individuals demonstrated the characteristics of more than one.

In his work, *The Republic*, **Plato** (428–347 BCE) described an ideal society in which each citizen had an integral role in maintaining social order. Although Plato was not interested in temperament, the social roles he defined are closely related to the humours of Hippocrates:

- Rationals were the thinkers and logical investigators.
- Guardians were the caretakers and lawmakers because of their practicality and common sense.
- Idealists were intuitive and sensitive and, therefore, took care of society's morals and ethics.
- Artisans were the makers and doers of all things artful and practical.

Plato's student, **Aristotle** (384–322 BCE) defined human temperament according to what made people happiest. Dialectical types found happiness in logical investigation and figuring things out. Proprietary types found happiness in acquiring money, possessions, and assets to ensure security. Ethical types were happiest when practising high morals and studying ethics. The Hedonic types found their happiness in sensual and tactile pleasures.

Galen (129 AD–c. 216) was a Greek physician, writer, and philosopher whose theories influenced European medicine for 1,500 years. He also built on the work of Hippocrates, developing the following categories to define the four personality types still used today.

Sanguine personalities are extroverts; they enjoy socialising with others, and they are forward and blunt in their opinions. After actively engaging with the outside world, sanguines often need alone time to regroup and recharge. They may spend this time on creative endeavours or hobbies. Sanguines are very passionate about their personal interests, but they are also easily distracted by new hobbies, people, or projects. When faced with a potentially stressful situation, sanguines can become emotional.

Phlegmatic personalities are almost the exact opposite of sanguines. While phlegmatics are friendly, their laid-back, introverted demeanour may make them seem unapproachable. This isn't so. Phlegmatics are shy and prefer to stay in situations that are comfortable to them rather than continually seeking out change and new experiences. Phlegmatics handle stressful situations best because they are rational, calm, and stable.

Choleric personalities are natural-born leaders and go-getters. Cholerics rarely sit on a couch watching television. Charismatic and full of energy, they often organise events, encourage others to reach their full potential, and delegate work. Since cholerics like to get things done, they may come across as being demanding, impatient, or bossy. They also tend to compartmentalise. This can be an asset in the workplace. But when this trait shows up in personal relationships, a choleric personality may come across as detached, insensitive, or rude.

Melancholic personalities are the most introverted of the four temperaments. Melancholics enjoy an independent lifestyle, often preferring to be alone. Melancholics are thinkers—they analyse events ad nauseam—which sometimes makes them indecisive and weighs them down with the fear they will make a less-than-perfect decision. While melancholics are picky about those with whom they associate, once they have forged a friendship, they are fiercely loyal and expect the same in return.

To sum up, almost all models divide people into four categories, and each category defines a certain personality type. Most of the research has been conducted independently over thousands of years and leads to a dominant pattern. Here is a recap of the four main types.

Type 1

- Achieves a sense of control through direct action that creates harmony and reduces dissonance; looks to the future to seek necessary actions.
- Achieves a sense of identity through inspiring others to align with their beliefs.
- Considers alignment, harmony, and perfection to be critical values.

Type 2

- Achieves a sense of control through exploration and problem solving.
- Achieves a sense of identity through independence and standing out.
- Considers freedom, innovation, and risk-taking to be critical values.

Type 3

- Achieves a sense of control through analysis and understanding.
- Achieves a sense of identity through designing and creating.
- Considers rationality and originality to be critical values.

Type 4

- Achieves a sense of control through making changes that affect others.
- Achieves a sense of identity through self-expression and inspiring others.
- Considers harmony and vision to be critical values.

The modern era

So, thousands of years of research and experience have resulted in the same conclusion: there are four main behavioural styles in the world, and we are all a combination of one, two, or all of them.

In modern times, the most famous scholar to continue this research was the Swiss psychiatrist, **Carl G. Jung** (1875–1961). Jung developed the theory of psychological type. He proposed that what appears to be random behaviour is the result of differences in the way people prefer to use their mental capacities. He observed people generally engage in one of two mental functions:

- Taking in information, which Jung called **perceiving**, or
- Organising information and coming to conclusions, which he called **judging**.

Additionally, Jung saw people preferring to perform each function in one of two ways. These are called **preferences,** and they fall into categories: Introvert/Extrovert, Intuiting/Thinking, Sensing/Feeling, and Judging/Perceiving. In 1921, Jung published *Psychological Types*, which outlined these preferences and categories, and served as the basis for the Myers-Briggs Type Indicator.

In 1928, the American psychologist and inventor, **William Moulton Marston** (May 9, 1893–May 2, 1947) published *Emotions* *of Normal People.* This book forms the theoretical basis for the DISC Model of Behaviour. Like his predecessors in the field, Marston suggested the behavioural expression of emotions could be categorised into four primary types, stemming from the person's perceptions of self in relationship to his or her environment. He labelled these four types Dominance (D), Inducement (I), Submission (S), and Compliance (C).

Marston's work focused on directly observable and measurable psychological phenomena. He was interested in using practical explanations to help people understand and manage their experiences and relationships. He also studied how a person's behaviour might change over time.

DISC came, by design, from Marston's search for measurements of the energy of behaviour and consciousness. Marston did not develop an assessment or test from his model, although others eventually did. He did, however, apply his model and theory in the real world when he consulted with Universal Studios in 1930 to help them transition from melodramatic silent pictures to movies with audio.

Walter V. Clarke (1894–1944), an industrial psychologist from the USA, was the first person to build an assessment instrument—a personality profile test—using Marston's theories, even though that was not his initial intent. Clarke observed some employees were successful and others failed even when they had similar educational backgrounds and work experience. The reason was almost always due to behaviour.

Clarke decided to create a psychometric model to measure the workplace behaviours of individuals and also the behavioural requirements of positions. The premise behind his work was simple: if employees were able to be themselves, they would be more successful on the job, and both the employee and the company would benefit.

In 1956, he published the "Activity Vector Analysis", a list of descriptors. He instructed people to mark the descriptors with which they could identify. The tool was intended for personnel selection by businesses. The four factors in his data—aggressive, sociable, stable, and avoidant—were based on Marston's model.

About ten years later, Walter Clarke Associates developed a new version of this instrument. It was called "Self-Description". Instead of using a checklist, this test required respondents to make a choice between two or more terms. Factor analysis of this assessment added to the support of a DISC-based instrument.

The **DISC model** identifies four dimensions of behaviour:

- **Dominance:** People with a D behavioural tendency seek to shape their environment by overcoming opposition to accomplish results.
- **Influence:** People with an I behavioural tendency seek to shape their environment by influencing or persuading others.
- **Steadiness:** People with an S behavioural tendency seek to cooperate with others to carry out their tasks.
- **Conscientiousness:** People with a C behavioural tendency seek to work within existing circumstances to ensure quality and accuracy.

There are hundreds of books on DISC. My favourite one is *Communication Skills Magic* by E.G. Sebastian. It is practical, funny, and enjoyable. Sebastian's book is a must read.

Just a note: Different DISC models use different names for each quadrant, sometimes different colours, or even their locations on the disc itself, so things can get confusing. As a rule, a name starting with *D* is going to be D style. In the section that follows, I am going to use the ICQ Global version, which is based on the strengths the types bring to a team.

1. D Style—Direction

These individuals are quite easy to recognise due to their high drive, outspoken nature, and tendency to be fast paced. They are goal oriented and know exactly what they want, and they go for it with 100% commitment and energy.

When interacting with those around them, D people tend to be outspoken, opinionated, pushy, and often have an explosive temper. They are frequently so focused on accomplishing their goals they neglect to listen to those around them or spend time on nurturing those relationships.

They are great at seeing the big picture and are excellent problem solvers. They prefer working individually and perform best in high-speed environments in which they can use their goal-setting and problem-solving skills.

Unfortunately, their 'just do it and do it now!' attitude often leads to task-hopping. And some of the activities they start never get finished. At times, due to their high speed and drive for quick completion, they fail to produce high-quality outcomes.

Main drive: Setting and accomplishing goals

Value to the team: They are doers—true go-getters—who do not waste time on chitchat. If we want a task accomplished or a challenge solved, give it to them.

D types are likely to
- feel they have absolute control over their environment
- enjoy competition and facing challenges
- get lots of things done each day
- take risks and challenge the status quo
- get angry quickly but also get over it quickly
- prefer being in charge
- shun people who resist change
- object to being told what to do
- become impatient with people who 'waste time' by planning ahead
- set high performance standards for themselves and others
- be confident in their ability to produce results
- make quick decisions
- become easily bored
- be overly blunt and oblivious to the feelings of others

D types excel at
- being bold and adventurous
- functioning in competitive environments
- taking on challenges
- getting things done on their own or as leaders
- leading a team towards achieving goals or beating the competition

D types are motivated by
- competition and winning
- being in charge
- taking on new opportunities and challenges
- being able to control their destiny
- having the authority to determine how things are done

- functioning in a rapidly paced, results-oriented environment
- success

D types are discouraged by
- others questioning them about their decisions
- being placed in a position in which they lack the power and authority to impact results
- finding themselves restricted to routine or repetitive tasks
- being put in a position of vulnerability
- limited access to necessary resources
- being monitored closely or micromanaged

Under stress, D types may
- quickly make irrational and reckless decisions
- be overly blunt, rude, or verbally abusive
- erupt in anger
- become extremely demanding and critical of others
- 'blow up' if they don't get their way
- tend to become bullies and 'run over' people

To achieve their greatest potential, D types should
- seek the input of others and demonstrate they value their opinions
- step back and consider potential outcomes before making critical decisions
- make an effort to explain their reasoning and gain 'buy-in' rather than simply stating decisions
- cultivate a higher level of tolerance and patience
- develop greater appreciation for the value of cooperation

D types are recognisable because they
- are extroverted, self-confident, and forceful
- focus on tasks and results much more than on people

- are risk-takers
- are usually impatient and in a hurry
- like to take control of discussions and meetings
- tend to be highly active and results oriented
- often speak loudly and interrupt others
- get to the point quickly

2. I Style—Inspiration

These individuals are the easiest to recognise due to their constantly upbeat nature, tireless enthusiasm, tendency to use humour, and great love of socialising.

I types are born talkers who have great verbal skills and excel at inspiring, influencing, and persuading others. They develop friendships easily and are great networkers. Their main goal in life is to inspire and entertain others. When people don't want to be entertained, I types often end up goofing around just to entertain themselves. They are born optimists who often overestimate their own abilities and the abilities of others. They can be enthusiastic about others' accomplishments or potential accomplishments and verbally reward them with an overabundance of praise.

I types prefer a work environment where they can use their great verbal and people skills. They often make decisions impulsively, and they frequently base those decisions on feelings rather than on facts and data.

When they have to complete a task, they have rather short attention spans. Therefore, they do best when assigned activities that can be completed in a short time and have the potential to produce immediate results. They are often so focused on socialising they can become a bit disorganised, both in their general work area and in scheduling tasks and appointments.

Main drive: Popularity and feeling appreciated

Value to the team: They often act for a team as lubricating oil acts for an engine. They make sure everyone is engaged and happy, often trying to inspire others to act. In fact, they do a better job at inspiring others to take action than actually taking action themselves. With their enthusiasm and optimism, they keep the morale of the team high. When conflict arises, they are usually successful at defusing it.

I types are likely to
- be popular and likable
- feel they can exercise a great degree of influence over their environment
- enjoy telling stories and have no problem exaggerating a bit
- be extremely outgoing and the life of the party
- be 'people persons' rather than being task-oriented
- have an ability to see the big picture and help their team understand their role in the mission
- trust other people, probably more than they should
- energise, inspire, and motivate others
- like meeting new people and networking
- dislike details
- prefer working within a team
- break the rules: they feel the rules don't apply to them
- be charming and persuasive
- be impulsive and somewhat disorganised

I types excel at
- communication and personal interaction
- finding and extracting the best from others
- helping people believe in themselves
- creating passion for a vision, mission, or goal
- being inspirational, enthusiastic, and creative

I types are motivated by
- social recognition
- being the centre of attention
- exercising their creative abilities

- friendly relationships
- new ideas, new projects, and new experiences
- working in a fast-paced, diverse environment
- setting new trends and initiating change

I types are discouraged by
- being forced to work on long, drawn-out projects
- being connected with unfriendly people
- adherence to rigid schedules and tight timelines
- being required to work alone
- performing routine or detailed tasks
- negative or pessimistic people
- being criticised in front of other people
- feeling ignored or left out

Under stress, I types may
- become impulsive
- regularly overpromise and underdeliver
- skip important details to get something 'out of their hair'
- lack commitment and follow-through
- try to talk their way out of uncomfortable situations
- become excessively shallow and trite

To achieve their greatest potential, I types should
- resist the urge to be impulsive by thinking things through first
- learn how to assess people and situations more realistically
- develop much better control over their use of time
- cultivate a sense of perseverance and follow-through
- become more reflective and thoughtful
- listen more intently to what others are saying
- become more discriminating

I types are recognisable because they

- tend to move fast, talk fast, and are friendly with most people
- prefer spending most of their time interacting with others
- consider themselves to be humorous and enjoy telling stories, joking, and entertaining other people
- tend to get excited easily about new ideas and opportunities
- tend to be enthusiastic, upbeat, and sociable most of the time

3. S Style—Service

These individuals have a tendency to be friendly, helpful, dependable, great listeners, and at times almost shy.

They are easy to get along with and prefer to keep their environments steady. They like to know exactly what is expected of them and often become experts at completing a handful of specific tasks. Frequently, they develop routines that help them effectively and consistently complete these tasks. Because they have difficulty adapting to change, they can even resist and sabotage the implementation of changes in their environment. Giving them timely notice about upcoming changes, and detailed explanations about why those changes are necessary, helps them adjust more easily to and support the upcoming adjustments.

S types are not the greatest at starting new projects. But, once they do decide or agree to start something, they finish what they started. This is unlike D, I, and DI blends, who are great at starting new projects but often don't finish them.

They work at a steady pace, which can be viewed by others as slow, especially by the D and I styles. But, due to their focus on completing a handful of tasks only, they are rather effective at finishing what they started.

When it comes to relationships, they are the easiest to get along with. They are patient, supportive, and excellent listeners who are always ready to hear others' complaints or success stories. However, they only develop deep friendships with a select number of people around them, those they feel can truly appreciate their strengths.

Main drive: Creating and maintaining a stable environment, including developing steady and supportive relationships

Value to the team: They are reliable individuals who may work at a slower pace but always complete assigned tasks. Their approachable and supportive demeanour makes them great team players.

S types are likely to
- enjoy helping other people
- stick with the way things have always been done
- shy away from the spotlight
- prefer working on a single project from beginning to end
- work at a steady pace and be reliable contributors
- be extremely loyal and quiet
- believe they have little control over their environment or circumstances
- provide comfort, sympathy, and friendship to others
- prefer a stable, harmonious environment
- dislike conflict

S types excel at
- listening to and sympathising with others
- being responsible, trustworthy, and hardworking team members
- soothing tensions and stabilising troubled environments
- building relationships with other people
- being steady, tolerant, and persistent

S types are motivated by
- working with a small group of people with whom they can develop long-term relationships
- having clearly defined rules and expectations that rarely change
- cooperating with others as team players
- working in a stable, harmonious environment
- maintaining the status quo
- being acknowledged for their hard work, service, and loyalty
- focusing on one task at a time

S types are discouraged by
- competitive, forceful, or antagonistic people
- being subjected to criticism or allowing other people to receive credit for their efforts
- being judged or accused unfairly
- having to make quick decisions or implement rapid change
- situations in which they lack the support of managers or co-workers
- abrupt or unexpected change

Under stress, S types may
- become overly critical of themselves
- withdraw from taking any initiatives to move forward (passive resistance)
- feel even constructive criticism of their work is a personal affront
- shut down emotionally and become uncommunicative
- mislead managers by pretending they will comply
- stubbornly resist even positive change
- wait for someone to tell them what to do, out of spite
- try to convince others they are victims or martyrs
- become frustrated and give up

111

To achieve their greatest potential, S types should
- adapt a more flexible approach to their daily schedule, tasks, and routines
- become more assertive in their communication and develop the ability to stand up for themselves
- learn to embrace changes in their environment and processes
- recognise other people can't read their minds or know what they're feeling unless they tell them
- be less accommodating of others' wants and needs and work on developing better prioritisation skills
- become more decisive and expedite their decision-making processes

S types are recognisable because they
- prefer to participate as supportive team members, not as leaders
- speak slowly and casually
- tend to be reserved, indirect, and informal
- like working with others in small, intimate groups
- are excellent listeners; people feel comfortable opening up to them
- rarely display their emotions openly
- place a high importance on other people and relationships
- wish to preserve harmony and stability at almost any cost

4. C Style—Competence

These individuals tend to be highly organised, follow rules closely, and are usually very particular about their surroundings.

They are great at planning activities and are excellent at following through with whatever they set out to do. They are not naturally great at starting new tasks. They need to understand why they should get involved with something, how the new task fits into their current schedule, how it helps them move towards current goals (or distracts them). Finally, they need a clear picture of how this new task can be completed.

Before jumping into anything, they analyse in depth all available data and get started only when they can see clearly the task can be completed and it is worth spending the time on it. Though they can take their time to make up their minds (which often is perceived by others as hesitation), once they start something, they finish it. Whatever they get involved in, they strive for perfection. They work in a focused manner and take their time to ensure accuracy in everything they do. When working, C types do not like to be distracted and, at times, can come across as cold and unfriendly.

Because they put a considerable amount of time into analysing—and, at times, over-analysing—whatever they get involved with, and because of their total commitment to deliver excellent results, they strongly dislike it when their work or work processes are criticised.

They spend considerable time worrying about accuracy and quality of outcomes while also making sure all rules are followed, both by them and the people around them. And, they make sure they come across as competent and knowledgeable.

C types tend to be withdrawn and rarely express their emotions. Their communication is usually brief; however, they can be rather verbose when describing job-related processes. When in a conflicting situation, they tend to internalise their hurts and later take their revenge by withholding information from the other party.

Main drive: Planning and accurate execution of plans.

Value to the team: they are excellent at analysing all types of technical and other types of data as well as putting together detailed plans, reports, etc. based on their analysis. They are very detail-oriented individuals who can be trusted to complete their tasks with the highest quality.

C types are likely to:

- avoid doing anything if they are even slightly uncertain about their qualifications
- prefer to work alone
- feel they are controlled by their environment
- want to be right and accurate all the time
- be overly cynical and sceptical
- be perfectionists, demanding extremely high standards, especially from themselves
- approach people and situations in a diplomatic and professional way
- investigate every possible nuance and eventuality before making a decision
- foster a reputation for being precise and logical
- generate strategies and procedures that produce predictable and reliable outcomes
- try to discover everything that could possibly go wrong
- be a stickler for detail
- place a high value on knowledge and expertise

C types excel at

- maintaining stability
- analysing complex situations or problems
- being extremely professional in their appearance and approach
- challenging assumptions
- being fair, rational, and objective at all times
- maintaining extremely high standards
- being unwilling to compromise quality, even under severe pressure or time constraints
- gaining insight into issues by asking the right questions
- being tactful and diplomatic

C-types are motivated by

- having the flexibility to explore issues, formulate plans, and bring them to fruition

- being recognised in private for specific achievements
- gaining respect for their expertise and knowledge
- being approached in a reserved, professional manner
- having complete command of all relevant information and facts
- being precise and accurate

C types are discouraged by
- being required to participate as team members or collaborate with others
- being forced to cope with unexpected or sudden change
- being required to openly disclose personal or private information
- being compelled to analyse information or to evaluate consequences without enough time to do so
- being required to be involved in drama or emotionally charged situations
- being questioned or criticised, especially in public
- being placed in an environment that lacks high standards or stringent control of outcomes

Under stress, C types may
- isolate themselves
- become extremely agitated and reactive when criticised
- tend to be overly critical of themselves and others
- suffer from 'analysis paralysis' – getting bogged down from striving for perfection
- become stubborn, withholding information and assistance
- forcing their perception on others, instead of promoting their ideas

To achieve their greatest potential, C types should
- develop a higher level of interpersonal communication and assertiveness
- learn when good enough is good enough

- seek the opinion of others before making their final decisions
- not overestimate the consequences of being wrong; it's not the end of the world
- recognise they don't have to be perfect before making a decision or expressing an opinion
- understand it's okay to be a little spontaneous and have fun once in awhile
- foster more interaction, involvement, and team participation

C types are recognisable because they
- seek inordinate amounts of information before making a decision
- create work environments that are usually neat and organised
- prefer to isolate themselves when evaluating problems or planning strategies
- are generally reserved, quiet, and formal
- rarely express opinions or actively participate at meetings
- are extremely cautious and calculating
- think carefully and cautiously before speaking or sharing ideas

Why do we click with some people but cannot stand others?

Some people have mixed feelings about (NLP), visualising sleazy salespeople from a second-hand car dealership or TV self-help gurus. But NLP is based on the most practical techniques of psychology, and it produces results. One of the most important is the establishment of rapport. This is the ability to relate to others in a way that creates trust and understanding. It means we can see the other person's point of view and can help them to understand ours. We don't have to agree with their way of thinking, or even like it, but understanding makes any form of communication easier.

Successful interactions depend largely on our ability to establish and maintain rapport. Surprisingly, we make most business decisions based on rapport rather than on technical merit. We are more likely to buy from, agree with, or support someone we can relate to than someone we cannot.

Dictionaries define rapport "as a relationship marked by harmony, conformity, accord, or affinity. It supports agreement, alignment, likeness, or similarity." There are two ways to see other people. We can choose to emphasise the differences or the similarities between us. For instance, we can always find things we have in common with someone, even if it is just being human. Likewise, there will always be differences between us and other people. Even clones would have different experiences.

When we emphasise the differences, we find it hard to establish rapport. By emphasising commonalities, resistance and antagonism generally disappear and cooperation improves. With practice, it becomes easy to find what we share with other people and to focus on it.

This book is not about NLP, but NLP helps to explain why it is crucial to adjust our behavioural and communication style, especially in a business context. The following is a discussion of a few techniques; it is not intended to be exhaustive.

Rapport is established and maintained by **pacing**. Pacing is the process of matching another person's behaviour, for example:

- **Body postures**: We can adjust our whole body, half of our body, or part of it to match the other person. If the body posture is unusual, however, matching can seem disrespectful. Subtlety is vital.
- **Breathing:** We can match the rate of a person's breathing, where they are breathing (chest, abdomen, or stomach), or how deeply they are breathing. This

117

is not a good technique if the person has difficulty breathing as you may feel similar symptoms.

- **Voice:** Matching the pace, volume, pitch, tone, and type of words is a little tricky to learn but worth it. If a person is talking slowly, slow down. If they speak softly, lower your voice.

Pacing shows acceptance of someone else by meeting them in their model of the world. It reduces the differences between us and others at a subconscious level. Once rapport is established, we can influence the other person's behaviour. If you would like to know whether you have rapport, make a movement and see if the person copies you. For instance, you might scratch your nose and watch for the other person to do the same.

Of course, if the other person is aware you are matching their behaviour, it becomes mimicry. Obvious attempts to copy people break rapport.

Another way of creating a deep rapport is by authentically trying to understand another person's **beliefs and values** without judgment. Once again, you do not have to agree with them or change any of your own values; the goal is to understand the other person.

This last paragraph leads us back to cross-cultural (interpersonal) communication. We talked about how we see the world through our own eyes and filtered through our own culture. Our values and beliefs are obvious to us. If you and I share the same principles, we are going to get along much better than if our principles differ.

Technically our values (WHY) determine how we behave, so if somebody behaves like us, we subconsciously assume the other person has similar values, and so we can trust them. That is why matching works. On the other hand, although this technique can help us build rapport, it does not guarantee we understand who another person is. Matching is not a replacement for getting to know someone.

Let me share a personal trick with you. Today, social etiquette is so strong and automatic it can hide peoples' real personality. When I came to the UK, this is what I found to be the most difficult aspect of cultural differences. In Hungary, if you ask someone "How are you?", he or she will start talking about problems, difficulties, etc. So, we don't really ask—if we do, we are truly interested. In the UK, people thought I was rude because I didn't immediately ask how they were. Okay, fair point. I needed to assimilate, so I did. Then, I was frustrated because everyone said the same thing without even looking into my eyes: "I am fine, and you?" After that, people would start talking or walking away. But, hey, wait. I was about to tell you how I was! Slowly, I realised this social interaction was no more than saying hi.

Later on, I realised it is not that bad. It takes two to play the game. When a shop assistant smiles at me or a banker offers me coffee, they might be doing it automatically—but still, it is much better than the situation somewhere else where, I feel lucky if somebody is willing to talk to me in a bank.

That is the main message of this chapter. We can learn best from each other. And, by adapting our communication style and behaviour, we can lead more enjoyable lives and achieve much more. I don't get upset anymore when I am asked how I am and don't get the chance to answer. At least we greeted each other, which is already an achievement. Indeed, there is something peaceful in this privacy, and to be honest, I find it very comfortable and efficient.

Once we establish rapport with an open mind and the right techniques, we can more deeply explore the dimensions of culture.

Let's now move on to the main cross-cultural models so we can learn what they are about.

CHAPTER 8

Culture: A Group Habit Driven by Values and Needs

"Strength lies in differences, not in similarities."
—Stephen R. Covey

I believe there may be more than five thousand definitions of the word *culture,* which can mean slightly different things to different people. Some of them are practical, some are inspiring, and some—such as the one quoted above—make us think. What is the right proportion of differences and similarities where strength lies? Is culture the existence of similarities or the glue that binds the differences together?

The following list contains various examples that highlight the concept's main characteristics. One is not necessarily better than another: they are just different ways of framing the same concept.

- Culture refers to the cumulative deposit of knowledge, experience, beliefs, values, attitudes, meanings, hierarchies, religion, notions of time, roles, spatial relations, concepts of the universe, and material objects and possessions acquired by a group of people in the course of generations through individual and group striving.

- Culture is the system of knowledge shared by a relatively large group of people.
- Culture is communication; communication is culture.
- Culture, in its broadest sense, is cultivated behaviour. It is the totality of a person's learned and accumulated experience, which is socially transmitted. More briefly, it is behaviour influenced by social learning.
- Culture is a way of life for a group of people—the behaviours, beliefs, values, and symbols that they accept, generally without thinking about them, and that are passed along by communication and imitation from one generation to the next.
- Culture is symbolic communication. Some of its symbols include a group's skills, knowledge, attitudes, values, and motives. The meanings of the symbols are learned and deliberately perpetuated in a society through its institutions.
- Culture consists of patterns, explicit and implicit, of and for behaviour that are acquired and transmitted by symbols, which constitute the distinctive achievement of human groups. This includes their embodiment in artefacts. The essential core of culture consists of traditional ideas and, especially, their attached values. Culture systems may, on one hand, be considered as products of action; on the other hand, they may be considered to be conditioning influences upon further action.
- Culture is the sum total of the learned behaviour of a group of people. The group's learned behaviour is generally considered to be the tradition of that people and is transmitted from generation to generation.

Geert Hofstede, the widely known Dutch researcher discussed in the next section, defines culture as "the collective programming of the mind which distinguishes the members of one group or category of people from another."

My favourite definition is the one I've used as the title of this chapter: **Culture is a group habit driven by values and needs.**

Based on these definitions and descriptions, we can infer the people around us and the environment shape us. According to this concept, challenges similar to those faced by our parents and peers condition us and trigger the same reaction in us, the types of reactions that work.

How is it possible, then, the same challenge can trigger different reactions? Shouldn't the same problem require the same solution in every culture? The answer is no, because event and reaction are related and depend on heritage and circumstances. One event can have multiple reactions as well. Have you ever been caught in the rain? I have. When I lived in Hungary, it was an interesting experience that I loved, especially in summer. When I came to live in the UK, it became a normal, everyday nuisance. In Thailand, it was shocking to get drenched in a monsoon. When we grow up in a place, what happens there is normal, and we learn how to deal with it in the best possible way by copying what others do successfully.

This chapter focuses on the main cross-cultural models that are the basis of any intercultural work. There are hundreds of books about this topic, so I am going to limit this discussion to four major frameworks that I believe complement one another.

Frameworks for studying cultural (national) differences

Hofstede's 6-D model

Geert Hofstede (b. 1928) is a Dutch cultural anthropologist and the founder of comparative intercultural research. Because of his numerous academic and cultural activities in different countries, Hofstede is regarded as one of the leading representatives of intercultural research. His theories and findings are used worldwide in both psychology and management studies. His most popular book, *Cultures and Organizations: Software of the Mind,* was first published in 1991 and has been translated into approximately twenty languages. According to *The Wall Street Journal,* Hofstede is one of the twenty most influential business thinkers in the world.

Between 1967 and 1973, professor Hofstede surveyed employees from multiple international IBM offices and found he could map national culture along five dimensions (later he added a sixth one). He rated forty countries for each dimension on a scale of 1–100. His concepts are still the most widely used in the field of comparative interculturalism.

Power Distance Index (PDI) is the degree of inequality between people, for example, physical and intellectual capabilities. This dimension expresses the degree to which the less-powerful members of a society accept and expect power is distributed unequally. The fundamental issue of this dimension is how a society handles inequalities among people. People in societies exhibiting a large degree of power distance accept a hierarchical order in which everybody has a place, and which needs no further justification. In societies with low power distance, people strive to equalise the distribution of power and demand justification for inequalities of power.

Individualism vs. Collectivism Index (IDV) identifies whether a culture holds individuals or the group responsible for the welfare of each member. The high side of this dimension, called individualism, can be defined as a preference for a loosely knit social framework in which individuals are expected to take care of only themselves and their immediate families. Its opposite, collectivism, represents a preference for a tightly knit framework in society in which individuals can expect their relatives or members of a particular in-group to look after them in exchange for unquestioning loyalty. A society's position on this dimension is reflected in whether people's self-image is defined in terms of 'me' or 'us'.

Masculinity vs. Femininity index (MAS) examines the relationship between gender and work roles. The masculinity side of this dimension represents a preference in society for achievement, heroism, assertiveness, and material rewards for success. Society at large is more competitive. Its opposite, femininity, stands for a preference for cooperation, modesty, caring for the weak, and quality of life. Society at large is more consensus oriented. In the business context, Masculinity vs. femininity is sometimes referred to as 'tough vs. gender' culture.

Uncertainty Avoidance Index (UAI) is the extent to which cultures socialise their members into accepting ambiguity and uncertainty. The Uncertainty Avoidance dimension expresses the degree to which the members of a society feel uncomfortable with uncertainty and ambiguity. The fundamental issue in this dimension is how a society deals with the fact the future can never be known: should we try to control the future or just let it happen? Countries exhibiting a strong UAI maintain rigid codes of belief and behaviour and are intolerant of unorthodox behaviours and ideas. Societies with a weak UAI maintain a more relaxed attitude—in other words, practice counts more than do principles.

Long-term/Short-term Orientation (LTO) was added as a dimension later. Every society has to maintain some links with its own past while dealing with the challenges of the present and the future. Societies prioritise these two existential goals differently. The ones that score low on this dimension, for example, prefer to maintain time-honoured traditions and norms while viewing societal change with suspicion. Those with a culture that scores high, on the other hand, take a more pragmatic approach: they encourage thrift and efforts in modern education to prepare for the future. In the business context, this dimension is referred to as 'normative (short term) vs. pragmatic (long term)' (PRA). In the academic environment, the phrase 'monumentalism vs. flexhumility' is sometimes used.

Kluckhohn-Strodtbeck framework

In 1961, the American anthropologist and social theorist, Clyde Kluckhohn, together with Fred Strodtbeck, Professor Emeritus of Sociology and Psychology, University of Chicago, developed the Values Orientation Theory, a model for analysing culture based on three principal assumptions:

1. There are a limited number of common human problems for which all people must find some solutions.
2. Despite the variability, there is a range of possible solutions.
3. All alternatives of all solutions are present in all societies at all times but are differentially preferred.

In line with this view, Kluckhohn and Strodtbeck suggested a society's solutions for its problems reflect its culture. Consequently, they created a framework for cultural assessment that includes six major orientations and asks:

1. Do people believe their environment controls them, they control the environment, or they are part of nature?
2. Do people focus on past events, on the present, or on the future implications of their actions?
3. Are people easily controlled and not to be trusted, or can they be trusted to act freely and responsibly?
4. Do people desire accomplishments in life, carefree lives, or spiritual and contemplative lives?

5. Do people believe individuals or groups are responsible for each person's welfare?

6. Do people prefer to conduct most activities in private or in public?

These are interesting questions we usually don't ask, because we take them for granted unless the social norms go against our own values. How would each of us deal with them? Do we blame or try to change the outside world, or do we assume something is wrong with us as individuals? Whichever option we choose, intentionally or subconsciously, it can create some serious friction in us.

Trompenaars and Hampden-Turner framework

The Seven Dimensions of Culture were identified by Fons Trompenaars, a Dutch organisational theorist and management consultant, and Charles Hampden-Turner, a British management philosopher.

The model was published in their 1997 book, *Riding the Waves of Culture*. Trompenaars and Hampden-Turner developed the model after spending ten years researching the preferences and values of people in dozens of cultures around the world. As part of the study, they surveyed more than 46,000 managers in forty countries. They found people from different cultures are not randomly different from one another but instead differ in very specific, even predictable, ways. The model concludes each culture has its own way of thinking, its own values and beliefs, and different preferences based on a variety of different factors.

The seven dimensions are:
1. **Universalism vs. particularism**: Cultures based on universalism place a high importance on laws, rules, values, and obligations. Rules come before

relationships, though the intention is to deal fairly with individuals. Cultures based on particularism believe each circumstance and each relationship dictate the rules by which people live. The response to a situation may change based on what is happening in the moment and who is involved.

2. **Individualism vs. communitarianism**: People in individual cultures believe in personal freedom and achievement. They believe we each make our own decisions and must take care of ourselves. Communitarian cultures consider the group to be more important than the individual. The group provides help and safety in exchange for loyalty but always takes precedence.

3. **Specific vs. diffuse**: In specific cultures, work and personal lives are separate. As a result, personal relationships don't have much of an impact on work objectives. And, although good relationships are important, individuals can work together without having a good relationship. In diffuse societies, work and personal life overlaps. Good relationships are vital to meeting business objectives and work and social relationships are basically the same. People spend time outside work hours with both colleagues and clients.

4. **Neutral vs. emotional**: In neutral cultures, people make a great effort to control their emotions and tend not to reveal what they are thinking or feeling. Reason influences action far more than their feelings do. On the other hand, in emotional cultures people find ways to express their emotions, even spontaneously, at work. Showing emotion is welcome and accepted.

5. **Achievement vs. ascription**: In achievement cultures, people are what they do and base their worth accordingly. These cultures value performance above

social hierarchy. In ascription cultures, people value power, title, and position, and roles define behaviour.

6. **Sequential time vs. synchronous time**: In environments where sequential time is important, people prefer events to happen in order. They place a high value on punctuality, planning, sticking to plans, and staying on schedule. Time is money, and people do not appreciate it when their schedule is thrown off. People with synchronous perspectives see past, present, and future as interwoven. They often work on several projects at once and view plans and commitments as flexible.

7. **Internal direction vs. external direction**: People who live in internally directed cultures believe they can control nature or their environment to achieve their goals. This includes how individuals work with teams and within organisations. People from externally directed cultures believe nature or the environment controls them; they must work within their environment to achieve their goals. At work or in relationships, they focus their actions on others, avoiding conflict where possible. People often need reassurance that they're doing a good job.

These dimensions seem more practical to me. Should I grass up my friend, or should I just follow the rules heartlessly? Should I respect your title and position or value your achievement? Do I respect inheriting money, fame, or growth? Even these questions might make your blood boil if the answers are so obvious to you anything else would be just plain wrong. That is completely normal. That is why people react so strongly when something goes against their values. Responding in an optimal way is nearly impossible unless we know why we are responding in a certain way and are aware of our own preferences. It does not mean we agree with someone else's preference; it means we can respect it and are able to see the situation from a different perspective. This is already a big step, and it's what we focus on during our workshops and coaching sessions when we do the Brain Fryer exercise. It is not the most politically correct title, but it sums up the difficulty of the task. I will show you an example later on in the chapter.

First, let's take a look at one of the most important models, created by Edward T. Hall.

Edward T. Hall's cultural factors

Anthropologist Edward T. Hall's theory of high- and low-context culture helps us to better understand the powerful effect culture has on communication. A key factor in his theory is **context,** which relates to the framework, background, and surrounding circumstances in which communication or an event takes place. The following widely-used example highlights the problems facing low-context North Americans when they interact with people from high-context cultures.

What follows is an icebreaker exercise we do at the beginning of ICQ Global workshops (I am not sure about the origins of the exercise, hence the lack of reference) First we ask participants to read the following dialogue:

Mark: Do you happen to know Suresh?

Ajay: Of course, I have worked closely with him on a number of projects over the past ten years. I know him very well.

Mark: I was thinking about meeting him and seeing if there might be a possibility for collaboration. What do you think?

Ajay: Yes, you should meet with him, and you should also meet with others.

Mark: Thanks. Who else should I meet with?

Ajay: You know, there are some girls who fall in love with a boy who is very popular, well dressed, and good looking. After they get married, they realise they made a mistake because the boy has no substance. Other girls will look for a guy with good character—checking out his family situation and talking with his friends about him. When she gets married, she is much happier than the girl who married the popular guy.

At this point, we check in with them to see if they understand the conversation. Usually the answer is yes, of course. Then we ask:

1. Should Mark meet with Suresh? Why or why not?
2. Why does Mark ask about other people to meet with?
3. Why does Ajay talk about a hypothetical marriage?

This is a prime example of two completely different communication styles: one that is direct and doesn't require reading between the lines; the other has the messages hidden in the context, not the words.

High-context cultures (including much of the Middle East, Asia, Africa, and South America) are relational, collectivist, intuitive, and contemplative. This means people in these cultures emphasise interpersonal relationships. Developing trust is an important first step to any business transaction. According to Hall, these cultures are collectivist, preferring group harmony and consensus to individual achievement. And people in these cultures are less governed by reason than by intuition or feelings. Words are not as important as context, which might include the speaker's tone of voice, facial expression, gestures, posture, and even the person's family history and status.

Hall recounts a Japanese manager explaining his culture's communication style to an American in this way: "We are a homogeneous people and don't have to speak as much as you do here. When we say one word, we understand ten. But here, you have to say ten to understand one." High-context communication tends to be more indirect and more formal. Flowery language, humility, and elaborate apologies are typical.

Low-context cultures (including North America and much of Western Europe) are logical, linear, individualistic, and action-oriented. People from low-context cultures value logic, facts, and directness. Solving a problem means lining up the facts and evaluating them one after another. Decisions are based on fact rather than on intuition. Discussions end with actions. And communicators are expected to be straightforward, concise, and efficient in describing what action is expected. To be absolutely clear, they strive to use precise words and intend them to be taken literally. Explicit contracts conclude negotiations.

This is very different from communicators in high-context cultures who depend less on language precision and legal documents. High-context businesspeople may even distrust a contract and be offended by the lack of trust it suggests.

Hall made another important and practical distinction in terms of communication.

- **Monochronic cultures** like to do just one thing at a time. They value a certain orderliness and sense of there being an appropriate time and place for everything. They do not value interruptions. They like to concentrate on the job at hand and take time commitments very seriously.

  In addition, monochronic people tend to show a great deal of respect for private property and are reluctant to be either a lender or a borrower. This is part of a general tendency to follow rules of privacy and consideration as well as a religious adherence to plans.

- **Polychronic cultures** like to do multiple things at the same time. A manager's office in a polychronic culture typically has an open door, a ringing phone, and a meeting all occurring at the same time. Though they can easily be distracted, polychronic people also tend to manage interruptions well, with a willingness to change plans often and easily. People are their main concern, particularly those closely related to them or to their function. And, they tend to build lifetime relationships. Issues, such as promptness, are firmly based on the relationship rather than on the task. And objectives are more like desirable outcomes than must-dos.

If you live in the USA, Canada, or Northern Europe, you live in a monochronic culture. If you live in Latin America, the Arab part of the Middle East, or sub-Saharan Africa, you live in a polychronic culture. Interactions between the two types can be problematic. Monochronic businessmen cannot understand why the person with whom they are meeting is always interrupted by phone calls and people stopping by. Is it meant to be insulting? When do they get down to business? Polychronic businessmen cannot understand why tasks are isolated from the organisation as a whole and measured by output in time instead of part of the overall organisational goal. How can you separate work time and personal time? Why would you let something as unimportant as a schedule negatively impact the quality of your relationships?

We can quickly see the problems. Recognising whether we are dealing with a polychronic or a monochronic culture and the attendant differences in how time and relationships are valued is crucial to being able to communicate effectively across cultures.

My question is, even if you live in a monochronic, organised culture, do you know people who are always late, and they have an obvious tendency for polychronic behaviour? Maybe even within your own family or circle of friends?

These dimensions drive individual behaviour as much as they drive group behaviour. The difference is the peer pressure within a group can be so strong it suppresses and modifies our behaviour; however, it does not change who we are, how we feel inside, or our preferences. What it does create is some serious frustration or disconnect in us, or between us and the group if we don't conform to the norms.

The Lewis Model

The Lewis model, pictured below, transcends these earlier works because the unit of analysis becomes the individual rather than a culture or a nation. Richard Lewis is a British linguist, cross-cultural communication consultant, and author. Perhaps his most famous book is *When Cultures Collide: Managing Successfully Across Cultures*. His more recent work, *The Cultural Imperative: Global Trends in the 21st Century*, incorporates his model of analysing cultures in terms of:

- **Linear-actives:** Cultures that plan, schedule, organise, and pursue one thing at a time (e.g., Germans and Swiss)
- **Multi-actives:** Cultures that are lively, loquacious, multitasking, and prioritise according to the importance or thrill of the event (e.g., Italians, Latin Americans, and Arabs)
- **Reactives:** Cultures that prioritise courtesy and respect, listen quietly, and react carefully to proposals (e.g., Chinese, Japanese, and Finns)

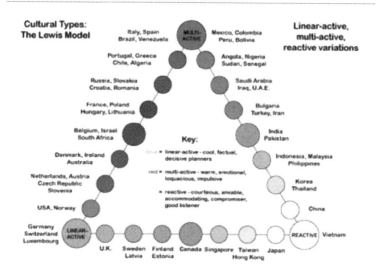

An experiential model, the Lewis framework is based on forty plus years of international consulting and some 32,000 interviews. Lewis spent much of his life learning languages and observing communication styles. His model has a practical validity to it.

Getting closer!

The CultureActive test, developed by Richard Lewis Communications, uses a series of questions to determine an individual's position within a triangle that shows the person's orientation to different cultures and, optionally, to his or her colleague if they take the test together. It is a useful tool that aids in the discovery of the similarities and possible sources of conflict within a team. You might think, "What does that mean, exactly? I understand DISC and personality types, but what can I do with this information? One of them talks half of the time; the other one talks most of the time. One of them confronts things logically; the other one confronts things emotionally. So, what exactly am I to do?"

I had the same problem and so did quite a few people with whom I spoke when I attended the accreditation course.

The Lewis Model was the first intercultural framework I got certified in because I loved its simplicity and the fact it is based more on behaviour than abstract values. One of my first workshops included a short session on this model as part of a DISC training. As soon as I finished, the DISC trainer asked me how the Lewis model was linked to DISC. I didn't know the answer, and asking the master trainers of the triangle model did not give me the information I was after. So I decided to find out.

My research led to the reconciliation of DISC and cross-cultural models. This was the first phase. Below are some of my original sketches. I mapped the above-mentioned models on the triangle using the latest high-tech devices—a highlighter and a pen.

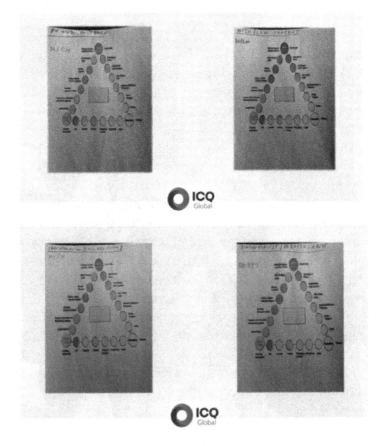

I used different colours for low and high scores of each dimension. The pattern is clear. It could not have been a coincidence. It meant different underlying values clearly influenced different behavioural styles.

We are one big step closer to the solution. To test it, I contacted hundreds of cross-cultural professors, lecturers, authors, trainers, and coaches to take my 15-question test and later sent them the results. Almost all of them were impressed by the accuracy and detail. They couldn't believe I could say so much about them based on 15 simple questions considering we had never met. (The two people who were not impressed said the test was a good one, but they did not believe in intercultural models. I didn't even try to convince them otherwise. They have their own approaches, which I respect.)

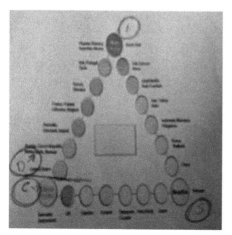

According to my assumption, the multi-active category relates to the I in DISC, the reactive to the S, and the linear-active to the D (countries closer to the multi-active side) and C (countries closer to the reactive side). This was a very good sign, so I carried on.

It became obvious the underlying values of individual behaviour are exactly the same as the underlying values of group behaviour, in other words, culture. Finally, it made sense. I have a personal preference for power distance and my environment has an accepted, normal level. The question is, is that preference higher or lower than other people's or the environment's and by how much. That determines how I see others and how they see me.

If the underlying drivers are the same, then it is possible to measure the intercultural/mindset gap between two individuals, two groups, or an individual and a group as shown below.

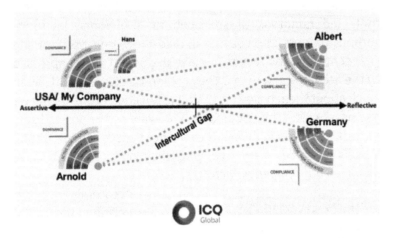

Following the same logic, there is a 'normal and accepted' behavioural style in every cultural group. For instance, in Germany the group would be more task oriented and reactive. From a DISC perspective that is a C-type behaviour. Does it mean everyone is a C-type person? Not at all. Does it mean a German D type would behave like one from the USA? Probably not, because displaying a dominant behavioural style in the USA is much more accepted and encouraged than it is in Germany. So, our cultural background can tone down and amplify our behaviour, but our preferences—the ones that determine what we need, what we want, and what we try to avoid at all costs—stay the same.

This type of test does not examine natural and adopted behaviours but preferred behavioural style and orientation from a cultural point of view. Why is it important? If an employer intends to hire a person or send one of their managers abroad, it is vital to understand an individual's personality can take on different behaviours. But individuals cannot suddenly change their core cultural orientation. They have the ability to behave differently in a professional environment; however, that does not mean that they change what they consider right and true, in other words, their values and beliefs.

I believe understanding and using different dimensions are important, especially if we need to prepare a country briefing or carry out consultancy on an international marketing campaign. This model can open many doors to interculturalists while giving practical tools to deal with cultures.

The main challenge in cross-cultural studies is to comprehend how other cultures think as a group; however, as noted before, an individual from another country can be the exact opposite of that group. Once we see how a person thinks, and add in their values and beliefs, we are on our way to knowing others, to influencing and helping them achieve their goals with a set of practical and modern tools.

As discussed in Chapter 5, **personality** refers to a person's relatively stable psychological and behavioural characteristics, the way the person views the world and relates to it. Personality remains, more or less, the same across various situations. That is what we measure, the underlying preferences.

Behavioural style, on the other hand, is the set of behaviours we tend to adopt on a consistent basis. When it comes to personality, scientists have not been able to come to terms with the years-long debate that centres on whether our personality is genetically imprinted or shaped by our environment. The truth probably lies somewhere between the two extremes: we are born with a genetic predisposition towards a certain personality, which is also shaped by our culture.

While we cannot really change our personality type, we can control our behaviour and choose to adopt behaviours that are most effective in different situations. And, through awareness of our strengths and weaknesses, and through self-control, we can choose to eliminate or redirect the behaviours that don't serve us in creating the relationships we want to create with those around us or that hinder us in our productivity and attainment of our goals.

Learning about values and beliefs is important, but we cannot practice values and beliefs—we can only practice behaviour. Practicing behaviour is easier if we understand the logic behind it, the underlying forces that drive it, and the perspective those forces give someone. The next section pulls all these approaches together.

PART TWO

Mindset Upgrade

The Best Leaders May Be the Ones Least Noticed
by Marshall Goldsmith

A lot of what passes for leadership development in companies can be a waste of time. See if you recognise this process. Your company taps you as a future leader. It sends you to 'leadership camp', which can last anywhere from a day to a couple of weeks. You're entertained by a parade of speakers (like me), and afterward you're required to critique the speakers and rate how effective they were. If the company is particularly rigorous about gathering information, you may be asked to critique the hotel and the food. But nobody is critiquing you. Nobody is following up to see what you learned or if you have actually become a more effective leader. As a result, the people who may be learning (and changing) the most are the speakers, the hotel staff members, and the cooks.

This is an odd thing that points out a huge fallacy about the process of helping people change for the better. We focus too much on the salesperson rather than the customer. We focus on the speaker rather than the learner. We focus on the coach rather than the person being coached. We focus too much on the leader rather than the people doing the work.

It's certainly true in my coaching. Of the great clients I have had the privilege to work with, Hal may be my star pupil. His co-workers judged him to have improved more than anyone I've worked with. Hal managed a division of about 40,000 people in one of the world's largest organisations. His CEO recognised Hal was a great leader and wanted him to expand his role by providing more leadership in building synergy across divisions. The CEO asked me to work with him. Hal eagerly accepted this challenge and involved his team. Together, they established the most rigorous project-management process I've ever seen. Each person took responsibility for creating positive synergy. They regularly reported on their efforts in reaching out to colleagues across the company to build teamwork. They kept learning from all of their colleagues. They thanked people for ideas and suggestions and followed up to ensure effective implementation.

And yet, as I told Hal, "I probably spent less time with you than any client I have ever coached. What should I learn from my experience with you and your team?"

Hal quietly pondered my question. "As a coach," he said, "you should realise success with your clients isn't about you. It's about the people who choose to work with you." He modestly chuckled, then continued. "In a way, I am the same. The success of my organization isn't about me. It's all about the great people who are working with me.

"This flies in the face of conventional wisdom about leadership. If you read the literature, you'll see that much of it exaggerates -- if not glamorizes -- the leader's contribution. The implication is everything grows out of the leader. She's responsible for improving you. She's the one who guides you to the promised land. Take the leader out of the equation, and people will behave like lost children.

This is hokum. As the ancient proverb says, "The best leader, the people do not notice. When the best leader's work is done, the people say, 'We did it ourselves.'"

"That's why I don't hold myself up as "coach as expert." I'm much more a "coach as facilitator." Most of what my clients learn about themselves comes not from me but from their friends, their colleagues, and their family members. I just try to provide help when needed and assist them in not wandering too far off the course that they have chosen.

For example, let's say you want to do a better job of listening. It's possible a coach can explain to you how to be a better listener. The advice will probably be reasonably logical, supportable, and hard to dispute. But it will be generic. It's much better to ask the most important people in your life, "Please give me some ideas on how I can do a better job of listening to you." They can give you specific, concrete suggestions that relate to them --how they perceive you as a listener --not vague ideas you can read in a book. They may not be experts on listening, but they actually know more about how to listen to them than anyone in the world.

I cannot make the successful people I work with change. I don't try. Too many people think a coach --especially an accomplished one --will solve their problems. That's like thinking you'll get in shape by hiring the world's best trainer and not by working out yourself.

Truly great leaders, like Hal, recognize how silly it is to think it's about the coach. Long-term success is created by the 40,000 people doing the work -- not just the one person who has the privilege of being at the top.

145

CHAPTER 9

Global DISC: The Blueprint of Why People Think and Behave Differently

"I don't like that man. I must get to know him better."
—Abraham Lincoln

Personality assessment without cultural Intelligence (ICQ) is like learning how to drive a car in an empty car park.** It seems to make sense until we find ourselves in busy traffic with roadblocks, cyclists, trucks, and angry commuters while it is pouring down in the middle of the night in a city where we have never been before.

On the other hand, if we vigorously study the traffic data of a metropolis, we have a rough idea about the average number and type of cars, accidents, and the scientifically validated proportion of pedestrians, cyclists, bikers, and motorists. We would feel fairly confident that as drivers we have a good grasp of the city. That might be the case until we actually face the powerful diversity of individuals who are nowhere near the average we expected, and it turns out some areas of the city are so different we cannot even recognise them. This is the challenge with intercultural (international) models.

People often say it is impossible to compare individual behaviour with culture. It does not even make sense. If we focus on the superficial layer, then it might be true. If we look at the deep layer, the cognitive one, then yes, we can. Indeed, we should, otherwise we cannot fully understand why people think and behave so differently, and most certainly it would be rather difficult to turn those differences into synergy instead of painful liability.

Our level of success is in direct proportion to the quality of our relationship with ourselves *and* others. It may sound obvious and simple, but it's not easy. There are a few reasons for this:

- Problems with false causes have no solutions. A lot of our clients want to learn how to manage and change others without realising leadership starts with them. If they are unable to lead themselves, they will struggle to lead others.
- Root causes of issues that seem to be a normal part of everyday life do not prompt people to look for ways to make them better. People are unreliable, difficult, and so on is a rational-sounding excuse to express the lack of understanding of our own and others' mindset.
- The symptoms of the current challenges are being addressed with solutions designed for the challenges belonging to previous generations.

Globalisation has changed the world

Companies can outsource any activity: manufacturing to China, call centres to India, IT to Thailand, marketing to Facebook, distribution to Amazon. They all have access to the same opportunities. Their people are their only remaining competitive advantage.

It is relatively easy to fix technology by optimising processes, but it is very challenging to work with other people. Statistically, three out of four people are significantly different to us in terms of how they think, make decisions, deal with conflicts, and express emotions. The quality of our relationships with others affects both our personal and professional lives.

Most start-ups fail or are not profitable because they do not understand how customers and employees think, what they want, and how they communicate. The highest-performing companies and most successful managers realise expectations, motivation, and behaviour depend on nationality, age, ethnicity, gender, profession, and personality type.

The science behind this is ICQ. It allows managers to measure and leverage personal and cultural differences, so their customers and employees won't feel confused, misunderstood, or disengaged, and then choose the competition.

Behavioural science has proven the most successful people are those who know themselves, both their strengths and weaknesses. This knowledge is important to them as they develop the strategies necessary to meet the demands and challenges of achieving success.

We have already discussed personality is shaped by both genetic and environmental influences, and it is partly inherited, partly learned, and often subconscious. 85% of people think they are objective; however, research shows 95% of our actions are based on unconscious bias. The mind filters an incredible amount of information through our unconscious biases, the little categories we try to fit to everything we see. The conscious mind is limited and tries to analyse this information while the unconscious mind starts seeing a pattern we might not even be aware of.

Our biases are influenced by our background, cultural environment, and personal experiences, and they have enormous impact on what we consider to be true and logical. The more we get this, the more successful and adaptable we can become.

149

That is exactly what **Global DISC™** has been designed for. It addresses all the challenges discussed so far in the book. **It makes the topic of ICQ uncomplicated and practical**, so you are able to recognise and understand the dynamics of individual and group behaviour and mindset.

When we move to a new country, we need a country-specific model to tell us what people are used to there. If our success depends on how well we understand ourselves and others, then we need Global DISC. This blueprint for why people think and behave differently addresses all three layers of identity. Not only does it consider national culture, but it covers the full spectrum of cognitive diversity.

Level 1—WHAT we do and say. This is based on standard DISC and visible behaviour.

Level 2—HOW we behave and communicate. This focuses on the five Global DISC dimensions, two for communication and three for behaviour.

Level 3—WHY we behave the way we do. This reveals the underlying values and drivers. Our values determine how we behave—they are our WHY.

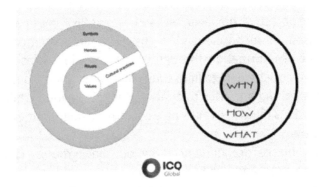

Global DISC introduces the topic of ICQ using the language of the most widely used behavioural model, DISC. It has already benefited some of the leading organisations in the USA and Europe, from start-ups to Fortune 500 companies, universities and government agencies, through a network of highly qualified licensees. It seamlessly integrates the most researched models and latest business data into a practical, proven solution. In a way, it is very similar to the smart phone example we discussed in Chapter 2. We seamlessly integrated the most researched models into one, practical framework.

Let's dive into the details.

Level 1 – Your WHAT

The only thing we can objectively see is someone's behaviour. Nothing else. But that is not going to stop us from assuming and 'knowing' why someone acts the way they do or what their intention is. Often we even assume we know exactly what they are thinking.

That's the challenge. We can pick up any behavioural style if we are skilled enough, so how do we know if somebody is being themselves or if they have modified their mannerisms to suit the environment and situation?

We don't. Not immediately. It takes time to find out.

Let's start with what we can see. Visible behaviour is what DISC is based on. The more we interact with someone, the more we are able to see who they really are.

151

As we discussed in previous chapters, **people behave in a way that supports their needs and reflects their values unless their environment forces them to act differently in order to be accepted.** That is exactly what we measure, **the mindset gap, the distance between what is natural to us and what is normal around us.**

Here, I'm going to digress for a minute. I had an interesting case a few years ago when a company specialising in DISC training approached me. A client from Brazil had come to meet them in Europe. They spent a day together during which it became obvious the woman was a hard-core D type. Nothing wrong with that. They agreed on what to do, and she went back to Brazil.

A few days later, one of the company employees made a mistake, and the situation turned stressful. But they knew she was a D type, and so they approached the situation from that angle. Unfortunately, the relationship only got worse and the company could not figure out why. That was when they came to us. I was able to show them something they did not expect, and it perfectly explained why their best intention backfired. As it is easier to use visuals, I am going to show it to you in the Level 3 section.

Our intention mostly depends on three factors:
- How we feel about the consequences of our actions.
- How the people most relevant to the situation think about the most likely outcome.
- How much we feel capable of and in control of the behaviour.

These factors are based mostly on our culture and personality (what we want to do vs. what we should or have to do). For instance, if I talk to you in a very straightforward manner, my intention is to get the message across efficiently and achieve the desired result. But, depending your experience, you might think my intention is to be provocative, rude, or aggressive.

You evaluate the intention, motivation, and values of my behaviour according to your own system and way of thinking, which is consistent with what you know, understand, and believe to be true and normal. This is where communication fails. The difficult part is controlling our judgements and assumptions by being open and having both the knowledge about other cultures and the skills to adapt when needed.

It is crucial to understand it is all relative. We need to appreciate how contexts differ. For instance, a very high D will find a very high I person annoyingly chatty and distracted, while the I person will be alienated by the D's factual, straightforward, and 'arrogant' style. **The level of frustration is going to be the same but for different reasons. What matters is the size of the mindset gap between them.**

Self-awareness is critical for personal and leadership development. The Global DISC assessment is based on your answers. If they are honest, you get honest results. It is not a test you can fail—it is an assessment to learn about yourself so you can take control of success.

The questions do not ask you about the values you like, want to project, or are used to. The survey should not take longer than 3–4 minutes, otherwise you might overthink it. The questions address what you would instinctively do or how you would react in a situation. They are not concerned with preference or how you want to behave.

For example, how would you answer the question: Do you interrupt people when they talk too much? You might be tempted to answer it depends on who you're talking to. That may be true, but how do you *feel* when somebody is talking too much? Do you have to restrain yourself and politely wait for your turn? In which case, answer yes. The questions have been phrased to put you in a particular situation; once you choose your answer, we derive the values that actually drive your behaviour and thinking. Follow your spider instincts while answering the questions.

Level 1 is pretty much DISC, and you can find it in any standard DISC assessment. What you won't find are Levels 2 and 3, the missing ICQ part and the range of options we can use the data for to measure the gap between two individuals, a person and a group, or two groups.

Standard DISC and behavioural models explain how the different personality types tend to behave if they are not influenced by anyone or anything around them. That situation is highly unlikely.

Level 2 – Your HOW

Level 2 is concerned with HOW the underlying values and drivers influence behaviour, and it is the bridge between your WHAT and WHY.

COMMUNICATION

OBJECTIVE	SUBJECTIVE
Linear, logical, fact-based communication focusing on resolving the task, rather on relationship. Highly individualistic, decisive, dry communication.	Spiral, more impulsive and implicit communication based on emotions focusing on relationship mainly. Group interest and harmony are important.

ASSERTIVE	REFLECTIVE
Conversation is as much about winning as exchanging information. While you respect people for who they are, your respect is earned by their achievement rather than their title.	Communication is about learning to see a situation from a different perspective, gaining more information and finding a better solution instead of wanting to be right. Social status and titles are important and respectable.

BEHAVIOUR

ACCEPTING

Bigger distance between bosses and subordinates. Parental management style is accepted or counter dependence is projected, less direct criticism. Group interest is important.

CHALLENGING

Consultative management style, free communication between bosses and subordinates, acting equal even without the power. Individual interest is important.

RESULT-ORIENTED

Focus on the big picture, ability to deal with ambiguity. Macro-management is more typical and ability to deal with risk in order to achieve results in the short run. Expressing emotions is acceptable.

PROCESS-ORIENTED

Detailed and organised style focusing on processes and stability. Micro-management style trying to minimise risk, slower pace. Expression of emotions is less acceptable.

OPEN

People-oriented, agreeable communication, sharing more personal information; social and professional roles overlap. Rules depend on relationships and situation.

GUARDED

Task-oriented behaviour, challenging attitude, preference for structure and results. Good relationship is not needed for co-operation, social roles are separate. Rules are for everyone to follow.

Our 15 Global DISC questions can generate more than 4,500 possible combinations depending on the answers you choose and in which order. Based on that, you learn about your preferences on the sliding scales pictured above. Our research shows a lot of coaches, trainers, and successful global leaders score somewhere in the middle. That's not to say those profiles are the ones to aim for, but they seem to be the result of experience and the ability to see a situation from different perspectives and adapt accordingly. If you score on either side, it's more challenging to understand why the other side thinks and behaves so differently. Indeed, why they think their way is the right one and yours is wrong. My results are closer to the left or right side. Maybe that is why I have always been interested in trying to understand people.

It's in this context the Brain Fryer exercise, as described in Chapter 8, is extremely useful, because participants learn how to switch perspectives. We present them with a range of situations or statements and ask them to interpret them from both angles depending on the underlying values and drivers we cover in Level 3.

The purpose of the task is to realise the advantages and disadvantages of both sides, how they perceive each other, and how they can turn their differences into synergy. This is not based on common sense and good intention. If that were the case, life would be easy and with far fewer conflicts.

Level 3 – Your WHY

This is the part where we introduce the topic of ICQ. Let's take the example of the Objective-Subjective dimension from the discussion of Level 2 above.

Telling someone the way they communicate is objective or subjective is useful, but why is that? What is important to them? What are they trying to achieve or avoid? How does it influence the way they see the world?

OBJECTIVE   SUBJECTIVE

People with a SUBJECTIVE style respect and are comfortable with communication that is complex, indirect, formal, polite, emotional, metaphoric, enthusiastic, or exaggerated. This style is found in cultures (S, I) that value Respect (High Power Distance) and Implicit language (High Context).

In **implicit** cultures, interactions are more abstract and indirect than factual. Team members value subtle language that implies rather than defines a specific meaning. You are expected to read between the lines and look for clues to what the speaker 'really' means.

People are expected to show respect for authorities and higher-status people. Formal language and politeness are often necessary, as is displaying appreciation for and loyalty to others. Friendliness and saving face are crucial. Subjective styles are uncomfortable or maybe offended by communication that is simple, direct, informal (rude), unemotional, logical, or critical.

Now we have some real insights. Level 3 deep dives into our core to reveal why we act and feel the way we do by going through all ten underlying values and drivers in the report.

The 42-page report (see Mission 9, called The Blueprint, in the Uncommon Sense Quest) is our own blueprint while it serves as a guide to get along with others. There is also a forty-minute online course built in using augmented reality technology. You can download a free app on your phone and then scan the icon, which unlocks the videos for you.

The report itself is very informative, but it comes alive when we compare our result with someone or a group. Everything is relative, everything makes sense from our perspective. Have you ever felt uncomfortable within your own country? Or do you often clash with family members or colleagues you grew up with? This part explains why.

Now, back to the Brazilian D-type client, and why the D-type approach backfired. Based on the information I received from the client, I had to believe she was a D type when she was in Europe. But what happened when she went back to Brazil and an I-type environment? Did she conform to the norms? Under stress and in new situations we tend to amplify who we really are, but when we are back to our usual environment, it can overpower us.

So, we compared D and I. The result was not meant to be 100% accurate, as it was very unlikely she was 100% D and Brazil 100% I. The goal was to reveal the intercultural gaps between the two styles, understand the underlying values and drivers, and come up with strategies to fix the situation.

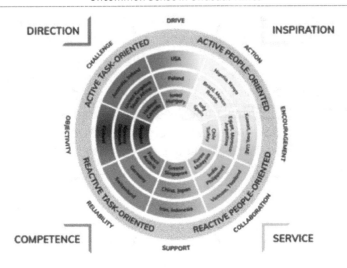

Global DISC country wheel

As you can see it on the Global DISC country wheel Brazil is in the I quadrant while she was in the D one. (The position of the countries is partly based on the previously mentioned models and partly on the 2014 Globe Study as the 'normal' behaviour styles in different countries are still powerful)

GLOBAL DISC™ DIMENSIONS

COMMUNICATION

OBJECTIVE

Linear, logical, fact-based communication focusing on resolving the task, rather on relationship. Highly individualistic, decisive, dry communication.

SUBJECTIVE

Spiral, more impulsive and implicit communication based on emotions focusing on relationship mainly. Group interest and harmony are important.

ASSERTIVE

Conversation is as much about winning as exchanging information. While you respect people for who they are, your respect is earned by their achievement rather than their title.

REFLECTIVE

Communication is about learning to see a situation from a different perspective, gaining more information and finding a better solution instead of wanting to be right. Social status and titles are important and respectable.

BEHAVIOUR

ACCEPTING

Bigger distance between bosses and subordinates. Parental management style is accepted or counter dependence is projected, less direct criticism. Group interest is important.

CHALLENGING

Consultative management style, free communication between bosses and subordinates, acting equal even without the power. Individual interest is important.

RESULT-ORIENTED

Focus on the big picture, ability to deal with ambiguity. Macro-management is more typical and ability to deal with risk in order to achieve results in the short run. Expressing emotions is acceptable.

PROCESS-ORIENTED

Detailed and organised style focusing on processes and stability. Micro-management style trying to minimise risk, slower pace. Expression of emotions is less acceptable.

OPEN

People-oriented, agreeable communication, sharing more personal information, social and professional roles overlap. Rules depend on relationships and situation.

GUARDED

Task-oriented behaviour, challenging attitude, preference for structure and results. Good relationship is not needed for co-operation, social roles are separate. Rules are for everyone to follow.

As you can see, in some respects the styles are very similar, and in some they are polar opposites, especially in the subjective-objective dimensions. What does it mean exactly?

They were communicating with her a down-to-facts manner, no fluff, no big words. Why was it a problem? Once we see the underlying drivers, it becomes obvious.

OBJECTIVE

OBJECTIVE COMMUNICATION

People with OBJECTIVE style respect and are comfortable with communication that is simple, clear, informal, unemotional, logical and reasonable. This is because this style is found in cultures (D, C) that value Equality (Low Power Distance) and Explicit language (Low Context).

SUBJECTIVE

SUBJECTIVE COMMUNICATION

People with SUBJECTIVE style respect and are comfortable with communication that is complex, indirect, formal, polite, emotional, metaphoric, enthusiastic or exaggerated. This is because this style is found in cultures (S, I) that value Respect (High Power Distance) and Implicit language (High Context).

159

When she went back to Brazil, she had to be an efficient, Brazilian manager because she was on display. Outside of Brazil, the factual communication style with no extra respect for her title, combined with the client's lower level on the corporate ladder, did not sit well. My suggestion was to change the person she was dealing with (that relationship was gone already) and let the CEO handle it in a slightly more theatrical way.

We went through the complete report, they implemented the changes, and today the relationship is stronger than before. Learning about personality types is great, but it is incomplete without understanding how our environment influences our behaviour. Mistakes are normal, and they happen. The question is how we deal with them.

It is not an easy process, which is why we wanted to make it as uncomplicated and practical as possible. It all starts with self-awareness. If we cannot lead ourselves, we will struggle with leading others.

Next step is to measure our level of ICQ. Is there an area we can improve in? There's an easy way to find out.

CHAPTER **10**

Bamboo Strong by Dr David Clive Price

"Notice that the stiffest tree is most easily cracked, while the bamboo or willow survives by bending with the wind."
– Bruce Lee

We are living and working in an age of rapid change: increasing globalisation and connectivity, faster time to market, more cross-border mergers and acquisitions, many new and more accessible markets, and greater mobility of workforces and teams. Even thirty years ago, we would have been able to more or less predict whom our business partners, suppliers, distributors, customers, bosses, work colleagues, and team members would be. We would have expected to interact with them safe in the certainty that most of them would be people like us.

Nowadays, these certainties are gone. Under the impact of migration, globalisation, and the concentration of work in super-connected cities across the world, we are dealing with people of many different national, ethnic, cultural, social, and generational backgrounds on a daily basis.

This means we are now required to develop and use a once neglected skill—cultural intelligence—as never before. The good news is that cultural intelligence can be discovered and forged into a powerful capability for success in the new global economy. Two decades of research by scholars in dozens of countries have contributed to the evolution of the Cultural Intelligence (CQ) Model, a simple and clear four-part system for approaching culturally diverse situations and the challenges of cross-cultural encounters.

The Bamboo Strong model offers a personal exploration of the CQ Model and its four capabilities—CQ Drive, CQ Knowledge, CQ Strategy, and CQ Action—together with a methodology for creating high-performing global management teams and leaders. The framework has been developed by Dr David Clive Price based on his own personal and academic experience.

Cultural intelligence starts with the personal—with how we see ourselves in different cultural situations, how much awareness we have of our own culture, personality, values and beliefs, and how they affect our thinking and behaviour.

The fact is, many of us are now global citizens of a world where multicultural diversity exists right on our doorstep and in all aspects of our lives, from going to the gym to shopping to dining out to using social media.

The Bamboo Strong CQ Model is intended to provide you with all the help you need to become a confident participant in cross-cultural encounters and to build relationships, communicate, negotiate, and lead across cultures both at home and overseas. Knowing the techniques is not enough. There is more to it.

Bamboo is a giant, woody grass that grows and transforms rapidly when it is cut down. It easily withstands the harshness of winter. It is incredibly strong and yet flexes and bends with the force of the wind or rain. That is why the ancient Chinese regarded the bamboo as a symbol of strength, courage, and resilience.

Cultural intelligence work is often complex and challenging. It requires patience, and nuance, and subtlety, which is perhaps why more than 90% of global executives identify cross-cultural effectiveness as their biggest challenge. If you have a black-and-white view of the world and of cultural issues, if you are impatient in new situations and fearful of losing control, cultural intelligence might not be for you. However, if you can train yourself to develop your CQ, you stand a much greater chance of success in today's global economy.

This essential capability is in even greater demand in a time of mass migration, religious fundamentalism, and a ready recourse to xenophobia and political demagoguery. The world needs leaders with high CQ (and ICQ)—not only to spread the message of tolerance but also to provide deeper and more nuanced insights into other viewpoints, conflicting opinions, and unfamiliar traditions and beliefs. It's easy to fall back on stereotype and intolerance.

The Bamboo Strong CQ Model suggests there is another way. It's a path of excitement and curiosity, of surprise and sheer delight in the discovery of other approaches and other viewpoints.

Courage (CQ Drive)

CQ Drive is your motivation and readiness to collaborate with others in a wide spectrum of cultural settings. It focuses on your ability to gain enjoyment from and reap the benefits of cross-cultural challenges in many contexts.

And just like the bamboo, which grows in phases marked by stronger circles on the stem, this is a process that can only evolve one step at a time, one cultural encounter at a time, as people reach out and flex their new-found understanding. The four capabilities of cultural intelligence—CQ Drive, CQ Knowledge, CQ Strategy, and CQ Action—are not individual and isolated aspects of our attempt to make the world a better place. They are interrelated stages in the development of our cultural intelligence and of becoming true Bamboo Leaders, whether you are a current leader or a high potential leader.

So let's look at these CQ strategies, to see how they can work together to make people like you and me better citizens of this new global economy.

Explore (CQ Knowledge)

The first thing to notice is that the different elements of cultural intelligence can be considered as stand-alone capabilities. You might, for example, be really interested in a particular culture or country (CQ Drive). And yet despite all your learning, reading books, watching movies from that country, and even learning some of the language (CQ Knowledge), you still feel completely out of it.

Simply having knowledge about a country or people's background is not enough to really interact with and learn from that culture. In fact, CQ Knowledge by itself might encourage a coolness and a false sense of control—like some of those academics, who studied Italian history but whose feeling for Italy was superior and distant. On the other hand, books, discussion groups, in-country planning sessions, videoconferences with global management teams and functions (CQ Strategy) can all help you prepare for the real engagement of joint projects and for CQ Action. The interaction of the four capabilities extends your repertoire of responses, behaviours, and ways to communicate with people from another background. Each capability encourages and reflects on the other, giving you much greater control over your life and work when dealing with differences and adding to your organisation's bottom line.

Perspective (CQ Strategy)

As we've learned in CQ Knowledge, if you're going to do business globally, you have to think not only globally but also locally. And that means developing your CQ Strategy as well as your CQ Knowledge.

If you or your team has low CQ Strategy, you won't be able to ask questions about new cultural situations, you won't think deeply about what might be going wrong, and you won't adjust accordingly.

On the other hand, high CQ Strategy will allow you to be agile in different cultural settings or in response to new cultural challenges. These may come from a multicultural workforce with diverse religious beliefs, your company's expansion into new markets, disruptive innovations and technologies, or perhaps from a videoconference with people from many different backgrounds (which is all too likely in our virtual world).

Responsiveness and sensitivity are what count—and you can't build this high CQ Strategy in one day. However, you can learn from the mistakes around you to develop your cultural intelligence skills over time.

Research suggests that exposure to a variety of cultural experiences in different countries, and an ability to adapt even when making mistakes, develops a much higher level of CQ Strategy than living and working in one particular overseas location – or indeed in one country and culture.

Those who are asked to react and solve problems in new cultural settings become, almost literally, 'wired'. And this can be true even when they fail in their first or second or third posting or relocation. Perhaps especially when they fail. The same applies to businesses expanding into new markets.

It seems that those with heightened CQ Strategy are able to pick themselves up and dust themselves off every time they fall flat on their face. And this resilience has enormous implications for business owners, SMEs and entrepreneurs in the multicultural future that is already upon us.

Performance (CQ Action)

Business dislikes ambiguity.

And yet uncertainty or ambiguity is exactly what many companies, entrepreneurs, and organisations face in this increasingly complex world of new frontiers, mass migration, and personal and cultural diversity. Companies want their leaders to deal with ambiguity.

New cross-cultural challenges present themselves every day in the form of an inexplicably hostile email, in the puzzled or unresponsive audience at a presentation, in a misfiring local community campaign. In almost every sphere of our life and performance we are required to think and respond with cultural intelligence.

CQ is a no brainer to inspire global performance, and so is the likelihood of failure. If you don't fail somewhere along the line, you cannot develop the higher level of CQ Action that this constant flow of intercultural challenges sends your way. The benefits in terms of performance often become evident over time.

There is no set process for acquiring perfect cultural intelligence or becoming a global leader or an expert in working with difference. What may have worked in one environment may well not work the same way in another culture.

What seemed the right strategy in one country may not be effective in another. We are often improvising, thinking on our feet, revising plans, and hopefully reflecting on what we are doing in our new cross-cultural encounters.

However, it is precisely because of these improvised situations, when we are suddenly called upon to react with sensitivity and understanding, that we should have a CQ model in place.

Thinking positive, being objective, stepping back, and observing are all useful pieces of advice, although if you have ever been really stressed, felt overwhelmed, you know exactly that it is really hard to do that and it is very easy to feel lost or trapped in the situation. The reason is not that we are not good enough. We are just in survival mode and that is not designed to make us smart, but to make us quick to run or strong to fight. The good news is that it gets easier as we practice. In the beginning we might need some help to speed up that process, and hiring a coach who understands this topic can save us a lot of hassle, time, and money.

I personally admire practitioners who get measurable and repeatable results. A prime example of that is Steve Jobs, the founder of the world's first one-trillion-dollar company. Even though his leadership style was not too people centred and he got a lot of criticism for it, he took it on board, admitted he needed help, and he got a coach, John Mattone.

John Mattone is the #1 authority in intelligent leadership and corporate culture with a deep understanding in psychology. He created a proven framework to bring out the best in leaders by understanding their inner and outer core so they can specifically target the areas where they need to improve.

The next chapter offers a short insight into his method and most importantly into the power of coaching.

CHAPTER 11

The Power of Coaching

"Have the guts to look inside and admit that while you may be good, you are not the best you can be."

—John Mattone

We live in a world where the word *apple* makes more people think about the iPhone than the fruit. Probably the second image to pop up is Steve Jobs wearing his black turtleneck on stage and then maybe his infamous leadership style. The story about Jobs' approach to management is true, and he was aware of it. Because he wanted to improve and become a better leader, he got in touch with John Mattone, the world's number one authority on corporate culture and leadership.

Together they used Mattone's model, the Intelligent Leadership (IL) Executive Coaching Process, to start their work. The model is a 6–12-month immersive leadership and personal growth journey that unlocks and unleashes clients' full potential, so they truly become the best version of the leaders and people they can be. It is worth noting we are not talking about a quick fix, a magical, intellectual hack to change identity and level up performance. The process requires hard work and commitment over an extended period of time.

I know because I have been using the model successfully for the past few years. John Mattone is a real practitioner, who has himself gone through the challenges the rest of us face in our careers, and he has a proven method to tackle them.

Different paths can lead to the same destination; you might use a different approach, which is perfectly fine too. My assumption is all models that actually work and get results have much more in common than at first is apparent. All are about understanding the blueprint of why people think and behave differently, and how to turn those differences into synergy, or at least minimise the avoidable damage clashes of common senses can cause.

Coaching is not just the privilege of high-performing leaders but is increasingly becoming part of their obligation towards their team. Leaders are both coaches and coachees who are developing themselves and others around them.

The good, the bad, and the "Oh, come on!"

Coaching involves creating exponential thinking by breaking down limiting beliefs, designing new visions, and crafting a strategic plan to make it all happen.

Everyone gets stuck sometimes. The key question is: Do they realise they're stuck and want to do something about it, or do they just accept the situation as good enough?

Let me tell you a story about a young man. We'll call him Tom but think of him a stand-in for me.

Tom was walking in the countryside lost in thought, when he got so distracted, he fell into a hole. The hole was so wide and deep, Tom could not climb out of it.

He could hear people passing by above him, but he was a proud man who did not want to appear weak, and so he did not call out. But when it started raining and the hole slowly began to fill up with water, Tom started to panic. He decided it was time to ask for help.

A doctor walked by. Hearing the noise Tom was making, the doctor approached and peered into the hole and asked if he could help. Tom explained how he had fallen in. The hole was too deep to climb out of, it was filling up with water, and he was getting really cold.

The doctor was very helpful. "Right, I see what your symptoms are," he said. He pulled out his notebook, wrote a prescription, and dropped it into the hole. Tom was surprised, because he had no idea how that was going to help. The doctor said, "If your symptoms persist, contact me again this time next week," and then he walked away.

Tom got even more nervous. He shouted out again, and luckily a counsellor walked by and offered his help. The counsellor started off by asking: "How does it feel being in that hole? Is it cold? Are you safe? What is your relationship with your father?" After 45 minutes of emotional conversation, the counsellor's watch started beeping, and he said the time was up for that week. Then he added, "If you still feel like this next week, give me a call, and I will be more than happy to talk to you."

Tom was running out of energy. He had been in the hole for hours, and he was about to lose hope. He tried one more time. "Please help! I have a problem, and I don't know what to do!" he shouted.

Somebody else heard the noise, walked over, and looked down into the hole—and recognised his friend, Tom! "Hey, how are you doing? How did you get in there?" When Tom explained what had happened, his friend jumped into the hole with him.

Tom was dumbfounded. "Why did you jump in? I've been here for all day and now there are two of us in here! That's stupid—now we're both stuck!"

But Tom's friend said, "Relax. I've been in this hole before, and I know how to get out of it!"

The challenges I have experienced and worked through might not be exactly the same as yours, but the steps and strategies I learned along the way can get you out of the hole. Asking for help is a smart and brave move. The challenge is to find someone who has already been through what it is you are struggling with and can save you years of frustration and missed opportunities by sharing their experience with you.

VUCA world is inclusive, everyone is in danger

Not even the executive suite is safe from the changes sweeping business today. In fact, the impact of those changes is felt most keenly at the executive level. CEOs, COOs, CFOs, and senior VPs—like everyone else—have to hit the ground running and keep running fast. Stockholders and stakeholders demand fast results. Teams must work more efficiently under greater pressure. High potentials and emerging leaders need to be identified and developed earlier and more effectively. Business savvy, which is always important, has been taken to new heights. Add to this the quest for job satisfaction and life balance, and you have the dynamic tension that creates the vital need for executive coaching.

Executive coaching is a professional process that links individual effectiveness to organisational performance. It is a strategic course of action that helps organisations attract and retain great leaders, enables executive teams to improve leadership and team performance, and supports senior executives responsible for making crucial business decisions and achieving outcomes. It truly provides the 'shock absorbers' for the ride on the often bumpy road of organisational change.

The powerful advantages in the leadership development process, particularly in areas where performance goals are at risk, have made coaching top-of-mind for executives and

Human Resources leaders alike. Yet there is still a tremendous gap between what is expected of executives and the resources available to help them acquire both the inner-core attributes and outer-core skills and competencies required to achieve those expectations. Executive coaching with the right tools closes that gap.

Research suggests that while executive coaching is a key concern for executives and Human Resources, only 35% of organisations surveyed in studies of executive development trends make use of executive coaching as part of their high-potential developmental programs. By comparison, almost half the organisations utilise executive coaching for their VP level and above executives.

For high-potentials, organisations continue to emphasise developmental job assignments and custom training programs as their primary developmental strategies. Two-thirds of the organisations surveyed do not cite executive coaching as an important developmental strategy for their high potential and emerging leader talent pools.

This is a significant issue, and an opportunity, for organisations, especially in light of what different generations expect from their employers. For example, Generation X employees want a casual, independent, flexible environment and a place to learn; Generation Y employees want a structured, supportive, and interactive environment.

Coaching needs for leaders at different life stages

Research has shown that, regardless of gender, younger executives in their thirties have lower levels of self-reflection than older ones, and the changes they undergo are less dramatic than the changes of older executives. Younger executives respond to specific guidelines and concrete recommendations, but they are less likely to wonder why those guidelines and recommendations are necessary.

Executive behaviour during executive coaching also differs by age rather than generation, which is consistent with previous research describing the ongoing maturation that occurs throughout adulthood. Researchers have identified three factors they believe account for differences among younger and older recipients of executive coaching:

- Younger executives often have the self-perception of being a 'winner' and are likelier to think of coaching as a perk that comes with being at the top.
- Younger executives have more difficulty recognising nuances of human behaviour and are more likely to think in black-and-white terms such as, "There is a single 'best' idea that should prevail."
- Younger executives are likelier to believe there is one right way to do things, while older executives are more willing to try different approaches.

You might notice these distinctions sound very similar to the cultural dimensions we covered in the previous chapters. This is not a coincidence: generations and genders are cultural groups, so their underlying drivers and beliefs can be objectively measured.

Making coaching work requires organisations and the people running them to prioritise coaching. Executive coaching should never be treated as an afterthought or an 'extra', but as an essential part of developing maximum leadership potential. At the same time, it's important companies do not overuse coaching or think coaching alone is capable of solving deeply entrenched organisational (or personal) problems. Coaching can be remarkably powerful, but it can't do the impossible.

Benefits of executive coaching

Executive coaching represents a powerful strategy for meeting the continuous growth and 'connectedness' needs of your future leaders.

That said, just like anything else, there is a lot of variability in the world of executive coaching. There are effective and ineffective executive coaches. Nowadays, anybody can call themselves a coach without having to commit to the continuous professional development (CPD) expected of other regulated professionals. Coaches are not legally required to be up to date in their chosen field like accountants or lawyers, for instance. Any coach can use the same title as those of us who invested several years in our education, and so, when a particular coach cannot deliver the results they promised, their clients may assume coaching does not work. That is a real a challenge for everyone involved.

It is critical to never underestimate the importance of hiring external coaches who have a solid 'operations' mindset and experience on the 'firing line' as operations leaders—on top of internationally accredited qualifications.

Building trust and empathy with high-potential coachees is everything, and having operations experience goes a long way towards helping a coach build rapport, trust, and credibility with a coachee. It is also crucial to understand the philosophy of the coach you are considering partnering with.

The Intelligent Leadership Blueprint focuses on leveraging the coachee's stakeholders and mentors throughout the coaching process. The strength and success of any coaching intervention is in direct proportion to how well the coach has created and facilitated a coaching process whereby the coachee actually learns more from their stakeholder and mentor interactions than the coach. The goal of any great coach is to create a foundation of continuous self-discovery and 'connectedness' learning for the coachee that endures well beyond the conclusion of the coaching assignment.

As shown in the image above, regardless of the application, Intelligent Leadership coaching follows a defined, consistent, multi-stage process that always promotes self-awareness, the 'will' to change, and the execution of attributes and competencies that drive individual and organisational performance to new heights.

Three major obstacles might arise before the process:

1. Leaders cannot admit they need to change.
2. They don't know how to do it.
3. It takes too much energy.

The goal is to help participants become who they want to become, not to tell them who that person is. It is about closing the gap between their real and ideal personality. People don't get better without structure and follow-up, so we need to get better at following up. We cannot change in the future, only in the present, and the simpler and more efficient the roadmap we use, the easier it is. It is a widely accepted fact we cannot outperform our own self-image, so working on that is crucial.

Changing behaviour without changing who we are is not sustainable. As Dr Joe Dispenza said, our personality creates our personal reality. It might sound a bit cheesy, but it does make sense. Repeating positive affirmations is not going to deliver positive results if we keep making negative choices while running on autopilot.

Leadership is a highly desired and often misunderstood profession just like coaching. Some people do it for the wrong reasons such as fame, money, power, being seen as a guru who hardly works, etc. Others grow into those identities to make a difference, bring out the best in people, and contribute to the greater good. Most people are somewhere in between.

How smart are we?

Coaching used to be a slightly negative connotation. In some cultures, it is or was almost a synonym for therapy. That is not the case anymore. Therapy deals with the past, coaching focuses on the present and future. That is where we can get things done. It doesn't mean something is wrong; on the contrary, it shows we are aiming for more than others think it is possible.

Even the best leaders need a coach, just like doctors need another doctor because self-diagnosis is often wrong. It's hard to see ourselves objectively, and talking to someone who has the skills to help us analyse our own situation, explore our options, learn from our mistakes, amplify our strengths, and make fewer mistakes can be invaluable.

It is my personal belief **coaching without cultural intelligence (ICQ) is incomplete and less efficient.** An honest conversation is great, but we cannot talk about something we are not aware of. If we do not know who we really are, what drives us, we won't be able to talk about it.

It is useful to dig deeper into our identity, and it is equally important to understand how our cultural background influences the way we express ourselves, what we consider normal, why we are not comfortable with being ourselves in certain situations.

177

I used to clash a lot with my father, and I found it frustrating when I had to work with him. I was not sure why, but I 'knew' it was wrong to treat people the way he treated me. Now, I know he scored really high on power distance, while my score is so low that if my cat is on the bed when I go to sleep, I will sleep on the floor, so I don't wake him up. He was there first, and we have the same rights.

Anyway, when I was young and unaware of the mind's invisible driving forces, I experienced the symptoms caused by my lack of understanding. One day, when I was working at home with my father, I mentioned my dissertation had been published in a book in Italy as a PhD study (even though I never even started a PhD). His reply was: "That's great, now clean up the garden."

I did not tidy up the garden, and two weeks later I was in the UK.

I do believe everything happens for a reason, so I have no regrets. Well, maybe some, because there was so much frustration and pain due to the different ways my father and I had of expressing similar feelings. Not to mention the years we have wasted.

Today I know he expressed his love the only way he knew how. Task-oriented people do it by doing something for you—working hard, fixing your car, cooking your meals. Those who are people oriented connect with you—they want to know how you feel or what is going on inside your head, and they want to talk. Because we can see only someone's behaviour, and we interpret their intention based on our own values and experiences, it is very easy to misunderstand their message.

Personally, I have lost important people in my life because we so badly misunderstood each other. We really wanted to make it work, we had the best intentions, but because we were unaware of the blueprint of why people think and behave differently, we struggled and hurt each other in the process.

The problem is not that we hurt ourselves, which is fine or at least acceptable up to a point. The real issue is when we hurt people around us while believing we are doing our best for them and ourselves. If you're task oriented, you can try make someone who is people oriented understand how important they are to you (which is why you have three jobs!), and they may understand for a while but not indefinitely. In their eyes, money and work are more important to you than they are. In yours, money and work are a way to provide them with security, safety, and the possibility of a better future. When they ask you why they mean nothing to you, you are shocked to the core.

This can or might have happened to you in your personal or your professional life. It feels horrible. What makes it worse is it could have been avoided. It is like trying to convince each other while speaking in different languages. No matter how hard we try, it is likely we will gradually run out of energy and give up, believing it was just not meant to be or we were incompatible.

Personal development feels like a slap in the face sometimes. It is not meant to be a jolly ride in the park, but it *is* meant to be fulfilling for you and the ones around you. Coaching and assessments that help us get to know ourselves are critical for success. We have to actively look for answers rather than just muse on what those answers might be. It doesn't matter how much we mull over how to say *bottle opener* in Spanish if we don't speak the language.

Smart people learn from other people's mistakes as well as their own. This book grew out of the serious miscalculations made by people who then learned valuable lessons and are passionate about helping others avoid the same missteps. Leadership, personal development, coaching, ICQ, and psychology are all based on the same concept. All lead towards very similar destinations, and the paths they take have much more in common than it may seem at first.

My advice is to look for coaches and trainers who have already failed and succeeded in the areas you want to improve in. Try to find those who have transformed themselves, their lives, or their businesses in ways you would consider both advantageous and fulfilling.

CHAPTER 12

Intelligent Global Leadership

"We find comfort among those who agree with us, and growth among those who don't."

—Frank A. Clark

Intelligent Global Leadership is a way of life, an attitude that encompasses everything we've talked about so far. It is also the name of the ICF accredited program we have developed based on the Global DISC and Bamboo Strong models.

We don't need a title to be a leader, as Robin Sharma made clear in his book, *The Leader Who Had No Title,* but we do need the skills to inspire and influence others and ourselves. These skills don't come naturally to most of us but are something we have to learn.

What is leadership exactly? What does global mindset mean exactly? We use those terms freely without realising they might mean something different to different people.

ICQ Global ran a survey to find out how others think about leadership. The answers to our questions offered a range of insights. Here are examples from people we have worked with:

What does global mindset mean to you?

- *The absence of cognitive biases when interacting and dealing with people and situations*
- *Being able to take a global view of the different cultures around the world.*
- *The ability to adapt to different surroundings, situations and cultures quickly without sacrificing core beliefs and objectives.*
- *Understanding different perspectives and backgrounds.*
- *Universal understanding of certain principles. A collection of best practices on how to live.*
- *Being open, empathetic, willing to accept other rules.*
- *The ability to see the world from another's point of view and to embrace our common humanity.*
- *Openness to learn about ourselves and others, willingness to move out of our comfort zone, recognising and integrating diversity and inclusion, adapting and managing different cultures, unbiased thinking.*
- *Approaching opportunities, challenges, people, and perspectives with the 'widest angle camera lens' you can to gain understanding.*
- *An appreciation of how to adapt global strategy and synergies to individual market needs.*
- *Society will need to instantly refrain from demonising management while at the same glorifying leadership. There is no place for this in modern and global leadership and management because they need to be one.*
- *Never assume, step back & reflect, observe local behaviour.*
- *Openness, Transparency and Cross Cultural/ Diversified Culture or Behaviour to perform, achieve and collaborate to create impact on larger environment and touch people's lives. It is a behaviour of Altruism which can impact Heart, Mind and Soul of People.*
- *A person who can easily collaborate with anyone from anywhere.*

- *Openness and empathy towards other people and values, other cultures, and other ways of doing things.*
- *An awareness of the implications of global cultures in how others make decisions ... or lead.*
- *Being able to think and speak in a language that will be understood by all.*
- *Hmmm.... 'Mindset' is word that bothers me, as too often it is a prelude to a conversation around right and wrong. Also how do you know someone has a particular mindset? ...Who gets to decide if they have not? What happens when a new one is needed?*
- *Interrelatedness and ability to respond intelligently to complex situations.*
- *It means thinking about what is best for all of humanity, not just the humanity in my borders (organisational, gender, race, country, etc.).*
- *Embracing diversity, intercultural understanding, following geopolitical development, utilising the potential, thinking, experience of the global organisation, being open-minded and interested, trying to understand before concluding.*

Eighty per cent of companies believe they have outstanding customer service, but only 8% of customers agree with them. How big do you think the gap is between how managers rate their own leadership skills and how employees and superiors do?

- *Along the same statistic as the example used.*
- *I think that there would be a 60% gap.*
- *Massive gap. Not sure how the question relates to customer service.*
- *About 50–60% difference.*
- *If you find one who is doing a very good job you cannot say they perform at 100%. Because there is always room for doing a better job. So let's say that's 80%. So one who*

does a poor job is at 20% because they do their best. The middle is 40%, so I guess somewhere around this figure there is the line of where people do a good job. But not outstanding.

- *Depends on the deep listening and communication skills of the leader.*
- *Big employees are afraid to tell the truth.*
- *Close to this rate but to a lesser extent.*
- *Huge, to my knowledge. There was a survey that stated that this gap was probably similar to this customer service one.*
- *I don't believe that managers automatically think they are leaders and vice versa. This may be two separate questions—that are unrelated to customer service. I am a bit confused here.*
- *Very significant gap. This assumes you can obtain the true view of employees. Many do not provide the raw truth in company engagement surveys for fear of their comments and scores being traced back to them.*
- *Leadership and Management globally is in denial. They still have the mindset that it is about them.*
- *Probably not as big as the customer service gap. However, I see an arrogance and a desire for power.*
- *The gap must be big, otherwise we would have more satisfied customers and employees. There is enough research data showing poor results. Poor results are often very nicely camouflaged by internal people in order to secure bonuses ... everyone protects each other for the sake of own personal interest.*
- *50–60% is the gap.*
- *The gap is very big I think. Leadership is quite a different skill from management. It means empathy, care for and motivating people. Not taking care of processes, which is what management does.*
- *The leadership gap between effective and responsive leadership and the actual performance of leaders (and*

the assumptions of HR departments) is much greater than it should be.

- *Similar. Just like managers have cultural lenses, they also have self-awareness lenses ... and blind spots. We see ourselves by our intentions. Others see us by our actions.*
- *I would say about the same.*
- *No idea, but big.*
- *It is all a question of perspective.*
- *People judge themselves by their intentions and others by their actions, that is, we hold others to a higher standard of behaviour than we hold ourselves. Does the growth in the pay gap between workers and managers in the last 30 years not reflect this? The monetary gap is a fair indicator or the size of the gap in perception and reality for customer service.*
- *At least 50% gap.*

The answers to the next two questions may explain why people responded the way did.

When I asked participants **how important it was to make people feel understood and engaged**, 78% of them said 10 out 10. Then I asked them **how skilled, on a scale from 1 to 10, the managers in their organisations were at making people feel understood and engaged**. The median number of the answers was 6, ranging from 2 to 10 where 10 meant they were very skilled.

How does that affect businesses? If employees do not feel engaged and understood, how would they treat your customers?

I know how I reacted when I was pissed off with my managers:

- I had some good suggestions, but a manager took credit for them. I kept my suggestions to myself from then on.
- I defused a potential complaint, but a manager ignored it. After a while I let things happen and only asked for the manager's help so he could practice his people skills.

- A manager asked me to do things that were his responsibility. I ignored customers as I was too busy doing double duty.

I am not proud of how I acted, but I was angry and frustrated, just like most employees worldwide. Leaders and employees do what they can get away with, what they tolerate from themselves and others around them.

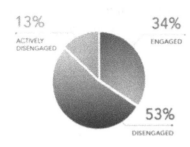

The statistics vary depending on the source, but they all have something in common: only a tiny fraction of employees is engaged, and the rest are not doing their best to support your business. Indeed, some of them are actively damaging it.

Mindset based on cognitive and behavioural flexibility

The message may sound scientific, but it's simply about bridging the gap between intention and action. How many people know the facts about smoking or being obese, and yet they continue to smoke or get heavier every day? The worst part is they want to change. They know what they should do, but for some reason they cannot do it. They are unable to influence themselves as much as they wish to, and it significantly limits their own potential.

Positive thinking and visualisation are not magical tools. Imagining and wishing for something better, while deep inside not expecting it to happen, is draining and disappointing. Working towards the best next step as opposed to the next best step creates momentum and builds credibility with ourselves.

If we understand the forces and dynamics of our own mindset, we can learn how to bring the best out of ourselves. There is no better investment than personal development and cultural intelligence (ICQ) is a crucial part of it.

It gives us the power to see a situation from multiple perspectives and choose the optimal response instead of automatically reacting the way we always do. Otherwise we keep getting the same results.

Leaders are masters of influence; they know how to propel themselves and others to move forward in life. In order to influence people, they know what already influences them. They know who they are, what their 'brand' is, and who they are to others. As a result, these leaders influence others to set a new standard for themselves that other people can live by. When you master the skill of influence as a leader, you control the ultimate force for giving, creating, sharing, and contributing more.

By now you can see ICQ is the science of uncommon sense. It is way beyond the habits and beliefs in different countries. It is a way to level up, or as Ed Mylett, the American entrepreneur and peak performance expert, would put it, a way to max out of what you are capable of.

From drowning in information to transformation

So far, we have gone through the strategies that help achieve transformation. What we are still missing is the answer to the most difficult questions we have to answer as coaches and trainers: "I feel inspired, I have the tools, but how can you help me apply that knowledge? What do I need? How would that feel?"

The answers are not as easy as you might expect. The process can be uncomfortable because it goes against our primal nature. Our brain is not designed to make us happy but to keep us safe and help us reproduce. Upgrading identity is uncomfortable, as our mind wants to bring us back to our comfort zone, where nothing grows but life is predictable.

Confidence is not knowing the answer to everything but understanding we can deal with whatever happens. Self-confidence is really self-trust. And, because 95% of our actions are based on values, beliefs, and memories we are not aware of, the more we know ourselves, the more trust we are going to have in ourselves.

There are three key ways to learn to trust ourselves:

1. We have to own up to our own story and be able to share it with others.

2. We need to be able to hear and process feedback about ourselves to reduce our blind spots.

3. We need to get passionate about getting out of our comfort zone, so we can learn new things about ourselves we would never discover otherwise.

We learn mostly from the reflection of our experiences, not from theories. There are three reasons why people FAIL to implement what they have studied/ read/ learned/ heard.

1. **Information overload:** If we have too much info, we don't use it at all. Pick the most important strategies to focus on, and let the rest go. At least for a while. People should learn less information more often, rather than learn more information less often. Spaced repetition is the key. Remember the padded-man experiment.

2. **Negative filtering:** A lot of people are so beaten down, they can't hear positive feedback when it comes their way, or they get defensive when they hear negative comments instead of focusing on the valuable lesson in them. We achieve only a small percentage of what we could, because we accept too little too soon, and everything is filtered through our negative thinking and our closed, judgemental mindset.

3. **Lack of follow-up:** Changing habits or behaviour requires concentrated effort. Without follow-up, learning gets lost. We must be willing to be mentored, coached, or taught. Lots of repetition, structure, and accountability are key to learning. The quicker we start practicing, the more we will master whatever we are learning.

The challenge is, if we try to change something too quickly, it triggers our reptilian brain and its fight-or-flight reaction. In the next chapter, we dive into how we can get out of our comfort zone without sounding the alarm in our head.

CHAPTER **13**

The Toughest Personal Development Course

"The way to love something is to realise it might be lost."
—G. K. Chesterton

The toughest personal development course is not a Tony Robbins boot camp or a one-week retreat in the mountains. It's being an entrepreneur, a parent, or a leader. There are plenty of companies and gurus selling their best practices, hacks, and tricks to influence others and scale up businesses if we subscribe to their special and exclusive mastermind group. Some of them might be worthwhile. Because I believe in the power of coaching and peer coaching, I have tried a few of them, too.

The fact of the matter is most of the information we need is also available for free online. Way more than we would ever need. The real value is in how business or life coaches synthetize it in a way we can actually apply it without having to spend years, and a fortune, on connecting the dots they have already done and tested for us.

I remember watching a movie scene between two friends. Both had been working in an investment bank and one, an architect in a previous life, had just been fired. Sitting on the steps outside his New York City brownstone, which he could no longer afford, the ex-architect began talking wistfully about what he felt his biggest achievement was: a bridge he had built across a river. I can't remember the exact numbers, but the approximate logic of the dialogue went as follows.

The bridge allowed people to shorten their journey by 30 miles a year. On average, 1,000 people crossed it every day. That meant 30,000 miles saved a day, 900,000 miles a month, 10,800,000 miles a year, or the equivalent of driving across the equatorial circumference of the Earth 432 times. If they drove an average 50 miles an hour, then the architect had saved them 216,000 hours, 9,000 days, or 24.5 years. Saving people all that time was actually incredible when he thought about it.

Sometimes we are not even aware of how much value we have to offer.

Title is optional, leadership is not

We don't have to have a title to be a leader or own our company to have an entrepreneurial mindset. If you are reading this book, then probably you are looking for good examples to model and bad ones to avoid. Techniques and stories are easy to remember, but habits are hard to change. Once we understand the mechanics of creating good habits, it becomes slightly easier. Then it's just a matter of practice.

As I mentioned at the beginning of this chapter, it is easy to find information, but extremely hard to undergo transformation. Reading a book or taking a course is not likely to change us, but finding somebody who holds us accountable, and who is committed to serving us instead of pleasing us, is a sure way of levelling up our mindset, life, and business.

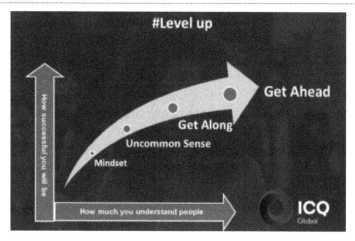

Step one is about understanding our own mindset, and getting familiar with the technology in our heads, so we can optimise it as opposed to just hoping for the best.

Step two is about getting to know other people's common sense, which might be disturbingly or pleasantly uncommon to us.

Once that is accomplished, it is much easier to get along so we can get ahead professionally. No shortcut, no hacks, no tricks. Step one is the most difficult as it forces us to face our demons. That is why a lot of programs skip this part: it is easier to please participants than to fearlessly serve them. That is wrong. As one of our clients mentioned in our feedback form, "There is no free ride here..." There shouldn't be.

Fix your thermostat

Human behaviour is like a thermostat, a very simple system with a sensor, a set point, and a switch. The sensor measures the temperature of the environment. If the temperature is in a given range, nothing happens. If it is below or above set point, it switches the heater on or off.

In terms of behaviour, this is called **perceptual control** (B.F. Skinner, American psychologist, behaviourist, author, inventor, and social philosopher) We act in ways to keep our perceptions of the world within acceptable boundaries. This is the reason why understanding how personality types and cultural background influence perceptions is critical for making sense of why people behave so differently.

At the heart of perceptual control exists a reference level, a range of perceptions that indicate the system is under control.

There are three kinds of levels to consider:

- **Set point:** minimum and maximum value. We all have these in every area of our lives. What do we tolerate? What is still acceptable? What is too much or not enough? Do we apply different standards to ourselves than to the people around us?
- **Range:** a spread of acceptable values, for example, how many minutes can somebody be late? What is our range? How flexible are we? Does it depend on context, or do we have a narrow range?
- **Error:** a value below or above the set point. It activates our system to take action. Think of the pain receptors in your skin. Most of the time they do nothing, but as soon as you burn yourself, they send a signal something is wrong, and you act on it immediately. This action is often instinctive, and sometimes we are not even aware of the reason behind it.

Cultural intelligence (ICQ) training means getting to know our own set points, expanding our range so it becomes less likely an error will trigger a reaction we don't want. On the other hand, people only expend effort if their reference levels are violated in some way; if their expectations are not violated, they simply don't act. A good book, a new magazine, a competitor can all be valuable if they reset our expectations and show us what is possible. This is why coaching and personal development are essential. Both can change our reference levels while giving us the strategies to level up, although it is hard to challenge ourselves enough and hold ourselves accountable.

One day, I had a coaching session where, as the coachee, I got a slap-in-the-face question to reflect upon: "What if you meet the ultimate version of yourself when you die? The one you were capable of becoming. Would you look like identical twins, or would you be ashamed and pissed off at how much you left on the table, or how much you let down your loved ones, because you were unwilling to push through your comfort zone?"

How would you answer that? Would you be proud and confident? I found myself silently blushing as I visualised the conversation between Csaba and Csaba 2.0. Shame and embarrassment rapidly turned into an internal rage over examples of me not pushing through my comfort zone, because I quickly found a reasonable-sounding excuse for why I deserved some slack.

The quality of our lives is in direct proportion to the quality of the questions we ask, and that was a top-of-the class question. Fear is often an invitation to get out of our comfort zone and discover our real potential.

That session led me to come up with more quality questions and reflections. Small wins can create the illusion we're being successful, so we start taking our foot off the gas. Moral licensing is a very likeable and dangerous mental glitch: doing something that helps to strengthen our positive self-image also makes us less worried about the consequences of immoral behaviour, and therefore more likely to make immoral choices. Technically we pat ourselves on the back for doing the right thing (for example, working hard all day) just to justify the wrong ones later on (I worked hard all day so tonight I can pig out, I deserve it!). The thermostat brings us back to normal.

Tiny little actions, but they all add up in the long run. Darren Hardy calls it *compound effect*. Jeff Olson likes using the term, *slight edge*, which is also the title of his book. Both talk about the same phenomenon. The slight edge philosophy is based on doing things that are easy little disciplines and, if done consistently over time, add up to the biggest accomplishments. The problem is all those things that are easy to do are just as easy not to do. Why is something easy not to do? Because if you don't do it, it won't kill you today. But, that simple, seemingly insignificant error in judgement, compounded over time, may kill you, destroy you, ruin your chances for success, and demolish your dreams. You can count on it.

If you smoked a cigarette and you immediately collapsed dead, would you ever light up another one? Highly unlikely. Smoking a fag won't kill you today, but compound all those chemicals over ten or twenty years and one day your stressed-out, overworked heart or lung just gives up. It's not the one cigarette, it's the thousands! That one smoke is just a simple, little error in judgement. But compounded over time, it can and will destroy you. It's easy to do! It's easy not to do!

According to Dr Joe Dispenza, the American neuroscientist, "Ninety-five per cent of who you are by the time you are 35 years old is a set of memorised behaviours and emotional reactions that create an identity subconsciously. Five per cent of your conscious mind that is plugged into reality is working against 95% of what you've memorized subconsciously."

We are creatures of our habits, prisoners of our comfort zone where we operate on autopilot and stop growing. When something does not grow, it dies, and that includes our skills as well. When we stop paying attention to what we do, we stop perfecting it. As leaders we cannot afford to do that. We have to stay relevant— indeed, we have to have a competitive advantage over those who try to take over our success.

Fear is the pain we feel when we push through our limits to expand our comfort zone. Technically the pain is good news because it means we are growing and becoming more.

Although ups and down in life are not optional, we may have more control than we think. If pain is unavoidable, the question is how we handle it and how ready we are to do that.

Growing through pain or growing through insight

There is a powerful concept in Zen Buddhism called Kensho vs Satori.

Kensho is growth by pain. When pain enters our lives, it can prompt us to make a shift. We may start a business that fails and lose a lot of money. It's really painful. But we can look back and try to assess what went wrong and learn what to do and what not to do when we start our next business.

Satori refers to moments of sudden awakening. It's growth by insight, which can appear almost at random. Think of those Aha! moments when something just clicks: an idea we picked up from a personal-growth program, a revelation we get from a retreat or a seminar, or the new wisdom we gain from a book or a meditation practice.

The choice is ours. Kensho is much more painful and unexpected; satori is more pleasant and controlled, because we are actively seeking the knowledge and experience that can take us to the next level. The earliest humans evolved seven million years ago, and their brains operated according to two principles: safety and efficiency. Our brain is three times bigger now but fundamentally the same, because almost any change is interpreted as risk.

In the history of humanity, only recently have we lived in a time where survival isn't at the forefront of the brain. Yet our brain hasn't caught up and is still running off a primitive operating software. To make things worse, instead of taking time out to implement a new software, we have simply downloaded modern updates on top of our caveman thinking system. Since this primitive system is more entrenched and more powerful, it is often the first to react to whatever stimulus we encounter.

Although we have an impressive array of emotions, our primitive brain relies on two networks for these emotions, threat and reward. All emotions derive from these two circuits, and applications range from someone cutting you off in traffic to someone mildly criticising our work. Most of these negative feelings and fears are based on old, real, or imagined memories. The amygdala is like a smoke detector in our reptilian brain, which is useful; however, there are many false alarms too. Fear makes us rationalise our way out of what we know we should be doing. The goal is to shift from 'fight and flight' to 'relax and respond'. **We need the negative focus to survive, but a positive one to thrive.** One does not exist without the other.

Biology gives us a brain, and life turns it into a mind. If we are willing to gamble and accept growth by pain, there is not much to do. As a leader or entrepreneur, life is going to throw out challenges for us, no doubt about it. The only thing worse than facing the pain of trauma is the chaos that comes from avoiding it.

Additionally, if we opt for Satori and we want to grow through insight, we are on the right track. If we take control and combine this option with some strategically induced pain, we have a winning combo. This is the approach we use in our programs.

The Quest to upgrade our mindset

If something is too complicated or boring, people are not going to use it, no matter how scientific it is, which makes it a waste of time. Our solution is a concept based on nearly forty years of research into behavioural change. Called "Do Something Different", the research is led by Professor Ben (C) Fletcher, founder of FIT Science, and Professor Karen Pine, Professor of Developmental Psychology, at the University of Hertfordshire.

Professors Fletcher and Pine have based the science of "Do Something Different" on three key findings from their academic research:

1. **People have different habits, knowledge, and personalities**. These differences should shape learning and development. Individual differences need to be addressed based on their own needs and values.

2. **Behavioural flexibility is essential for functioning in the world**. Helping people behave in new ways helps them to act upon their knowledge and intentions. Knowledge alone is not enough. Science shows the connection between knowing and doing is weak. The brain is a powerful habit machine that tends to repeat past actions and behaviours. This means a lot of training fails to get applied. When people are more flexible in

their behaviours, they become more cognitively flexible too.

3. **To be most effective, learning and development needs to occur in small steps over time and in the everyday situations the behaviours are needed.** It is not delivered in a classroom, in role plays, or in abstract. The changes happen in real life.

Not only has this concept been around for long time, it is also both robust and proven, and so we have applied it to the Global DISC program. We have developed an interactive coaching app called Quest to expand a comfort zone and dramatically enhance the behavioural flexibility of each personality type. It is the ideal balance of challenge and support, insight and discomfort.

There are three levels with seven mission (tasks) on each of them.

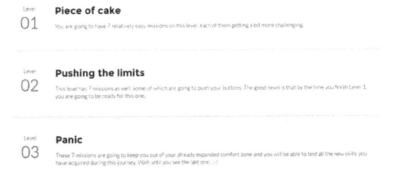

Level
01 **Piece of cake**
You are going to have 7 relatively easy missions on this level, each of them getting a bit more challenging.

Level
02 **Pushing the limits**
This level has 7 missions as well, some of which are going to push your buttons. The good news is that by the time you finish Level 1, you are going to be ready for this one.

Level
03 **Panic**
These 7 missions are going to keep you out of your already expanded comfort zone and you will be able to test all the new skills you have acquired during this journey. Wait until you see the last one. :-)

Quest is not a boring online course but more like the fight club, and you cannot tell anyone you are doing it. When you get your first mission, you need to execute the task while interacting with others. You do something different to what you would normally do, and you get a different reaction and a different outcome. After that, you go back to your app to answer some reflective questions and you can unlock the next mission. The tasks are fun and blissfully uncomfortable.

An individual who succeeds is invested in a program rather than a single event. Real breakthrough happens only if we follow through. For that to happen, we need to know exactly where we stand and want to get to. Once we have clarity, we find the solution.

According to research conducted by an Open University doctoral student, the average completion rate for open online courses is less than 7% meaning 93% of students who enrolled in such programs never completed them. At the 2015 IDPF/BE conference, Kobo (one of the world's fastest-growing eReading services) disclosed data that shows 60% of books purchased are never opened even if the content in them could save people years of failures and frustration.

This hybrid book is an invite to step up your game and adopt a mastery mindset and apply everything you learned. You cannot learn to drive a car by reading a book about it. You cannot become a great manager by merely going through case studies. Similarly, you won't achieve excellent results in your life by reading about raising your standards and developing a growth mindset.

The journey to greatness begins the moment our preferences for comfort and certainty are over-ruled by a greater purpose that requires challenge and contribution. This allows us to master the art of influencing others in such a way they feel respected, valued, and appreciated. No surprise: it stems from the same source—understanding the blueprint of why people feel, think and behave differently and the ability to bring out the best in ourselves and others.

CHAPTER **14**

Face Your Demons or Become One

"Action comes about if and only if we find a discrepancy between what we are experiencing and what we want to experience."
—Philip J. Runkel

Probably most of us agree real personal and leadership development is not a walk in the park but a never-ending quest. The question is how we approach it.

There are two main routes.

One supposes we begin from a feeling of not being enough and the sensation that something is missing. Success is reaching a goal that gives us a meaning of purpose and a deep sense of rightness.

The other suggests we have everything we need, but we have lost touch with who we are because we give so much weight to other people's opinions. Success happens when we get rid of all the unnecessary layers of habits and beliefs that hinder us from achieving our goals.

Either path can get us to our destination. Personally, I believe in the right combination of both. I need to face my demons so I can politely ask them to leave, and I also need to acquire new skills, knowledge, and experience.

The two approaches bear a resemblance to the six human needs or values. I picture them on a sliding scale where I have to find the balance between the two opposing forces. If I have the feeling of not being enough and have to desperately work at becoming more, that doesn't do much to help my self-esteem. If I assume I know everything, and just have to peel off the unwanted layers, I would feel like a fraudulent guru waiting for enlightenment.

Where I position myself on that personal development scale can shift depending on how much progress I make. My experience is most people start with the burning desire of becoming more and then realise they have much more to offer than they thought. This leads to wanting to use those skills instead of just acknowledging they exist.

When shame becomes a management style, engagement dies

This concept, which I came across while reading Brené Brown's *Daring Greatly*, was an eye-opener. Although she focuses on a corporate environment, my first thought was: "Oh, that is exactly how I managed … myself. No wonder I had enough."

Intelligent Global Leadership starts with the ability to lead ourselves. How we do that is vital. Let's be honest, most of us can be much harsher on ourselves than on others. The way I used to beat myself up was really nasty. Using a combination of guilt, shame, and maybe some disappointment and disgust is not helpful. It is a vicious cycle that needs to be stopped.

Let's take the example of exercising. Approaching working out today as a punishment for pigging out yesterday would be a strange way of motivating myself. How on earth can I create the body I've always wanted when I'm thinking of punishing it for being what it is? If we can't accept ourselves, we judge ourselves. And if we do that, we will judge others and project our own traits we cannot stand onto them.

We will be constantly chasing something we won't able to achieve, purely because we can't accept where we are in the first place. This is where self-inclusion becomes important, though it can be difficult to apply, especially in a masculine culture where we cannot show weakness and have no time for reflection. Vulnerability is weakness. Or maybe it isn't? For a long time, I thought it was. Then I read Brené Brown's book.

Vulnerability is uncertainty, risk, emotional exposure. If you can handle all that, you are strong. **Vulnerability means "capable of being wounded" as opposed to weakness, which means "the inability to withstand attack".** The illusion of invulnerability undermines what it is supposed to protect. When I pretended to be tough to protect myself, I ultimately made myself weaker because I refused to face my own demons, who happily stayed with me and got stronger. Not a good deal for me.

Projecting myself as being logical and strong was a lie, so I started reviewing my past. When I was too insecure to say I did not understand something, I did not learn anything new, and my lack of understanding was probably obvious to everyone anyway. When I could not ask for help, I wasted time figuring out what was available already. When I got into new situations, I was as curious and clueless as others to see how I was going to react. That was stressful. Sometimes we plan so much in our heads to make things perfect that it never happens or is completely different to what we so meticulously constructed in our mind.

We all know people who pretend to know everything, who always seem to be confident, and yet we don't trust them. So why would others trust us when we do the same thing? We are drawn to others' vulnerability and honesty, but we are repelled by our own. When we pretend we can avoid vulnerability, we engage in behaviours that are often inconsistent with who we want to be. It does not mean we have to share all our feelings with everyone; we only have to share with those who have earned our trust.

This book is about getting to the root cause of why people-management solutions are struggling to get the results they promise. It is easy to become passionate about treating the symptoms (disengagement at work, lack of motivation, conflicts, managing others). It is much more difficult to address the underlying reasons.

Facing our demons means we can talk about difficult topics. They exist on both individual and corporate levels. We already discussed the challenge of overdoing political correctness to the point where it takes away the possibility of finding a common ground as people have no idea what they can and cannot say anymore. Shame thrives in this kind of environment. It gets its power from being hidden. Political correctness is needed: it is polite and useful as long as it doesn't inhibit us from openly talking about difficult topics.

Shame can become fear, which leads to risk-aversion and self-protection. None of those outcomes is good for us or our business. When we feel ashamed, we tend to blame others or ourselves. According to clinical psychologists, not discussing trauma can cause much more damage than the event itself. Do you remember the story about the stressed-out zebra at the beginning of the book? How humans relive their experiences in their heads, which produces the same chemicals as the actual event? How much damage can it cause?

Why do we do that? A neuroscientist might explain it this way: because the feeling of shame triggers our 'fight or flight' response, and the pain we experience can be very much physical, we feel compelled to move away from that pain, even when there is no pleasure to move towards.

The good news is we can learn to use the concept of pain and pleasure to our advantage, and this is what coaches do. They rely on the hierarchy of pain by raising awareness about the amount of damage ignoring a problem would cause so the pain of doing something about it now would become less painful and we choose that.

The purpose of this book is to present you with different perspectives, questions, approaches, results and probabilities so you can make the best decision for yourself. This journey is as personal as it is professional. Much like personality and cultural background, there is no clear dividing line between the two.

If I've done my job properly here, and you also do your part, a few things will happen:

- You will have more questions now than before you started the book. That is a good sign.
- Maybe you disagreed with something I said so much that you looked it up and discussed it with others.
- You will have a better understanding of yourself and situations where you hit it off with someone but clash with others.
- You will be able to spend much more energy on what you want to create in your life instead of fighting what you don't.

I hope this book is just a beginning of your Quest or at least a valuable stop on the way. Don't forget to drop me an email with the receipt of the book to uncommonsense@icq.global if you want to try the assessment followed by the interactive coaching platform.

Enjoy the ride and let's stay in touch!

Eye-opening Reading

Digital and offline articles, researches

Cultural differences are more than countries: https://hbr.org/2016/01/cultural-differences-are-more-complicated-than-what-country-youre-from

80% of cultural differences are within countries, not between them: https://hbr.org/2016/05/research-the-biggest-culture-gaps-are-within-countries-not-between-them

Debunking diversity: https://www.entrepreneur.com/article/291066

Hiring the full range of colours just to blend them into your own: https://www.entrepreneur.com/article/327542

The higher up you go, the more your behaviour is important: https://www.businessinsider.com/toxic-personality-traits-ruin-your-career-2019-4?r=US&IR=T

Visible diversity has no proven benefit: https://hbr.org/2017/03/teams-solve-problems-faster-when-theyre-more-cognitively-diverse

Closing the interaction gap: https://hbr.org/2017/10/closing-the-strategy-execution-gap-means-focusing-on-what-employees-think-not-what-they-do

https://www.forbes.com/sites/rasmushougaard/2018/09/09/the-real-crisis-in-leadership/

Aim for inclusion, not diversity: https://hbr.org/2018/12/to-retain-employees-focus-on-inclusion-not-just-diversity?utm_medium=social&utm_campaign=hbr&utm_source=facebook

Execution gap: https://hbr.org/2017/10/closing-the-strategy-execution-gap-means-focusing-on-what-employees-think-not-what-they-do

MBTI tests 5 weeks later: https://fortune.com/2013/05/15/have-we-all-been-duped-by-the-myers-briggs-test/

Mindgym: https://uk.themindgym.com/solutions/management-development/

60-80% of all problems stem from strainer relationships: Daniel Dana, Managing Differences: How to Build Better Relationships at Work and Home (2005, 4th ed.); Barbara J. Kreisman, Insights into Employee Motivation, Commitment and Retention (2002).

https://globeproject.com/study_2014

Print

Adams, Robert. *Discover the Power of You: How to Cultivate Change for Positive and Productive Cultures*, Business Books, 2017

Alessandra, Tony. *The Platinum Rule: Discover the Four Basic Business Personalities and How They Can Lead You to Success*, Warner Books, 1998

Brown Brené. *Daring Greatly: How the Courage to Be Vulnerable Transforms the Way We Live, Love, Parent, and Lead*, Penguin Life, 2015

Bushe, Gervase R. *Clear Leadership: Sustaining Real Collaboration and Partnership at Work*, Davies Black, 2010

Chandler, Steve. *Reinventing Yourself*, New Page Books, 2017

--------------------. *Shift Your Mind: Shift the World,* Maurice Bassett, 2018

Covey, Stephen M. *The Speed of Trust: The One Thing that Changes Everything*, Simon & Schuster UK, 2008

Coyle, Daniel. *The Culture Code: The Secrets of Highly Successful Groups*, Random House Business, 2019

Degraff, Jeff and Quinn, Robert E. *Competing Values Leadership*, Edward Elgar Publishing Ltd, 2014

Dennett, Daniel. *Consciousness Explained*, Little, Brown and Co, 1991

Dispenza, Joe. *Breaking the Habit of Being Yourself: How to Lose Your Mind and Create a New One,* Hay House, 2012

----------------------. *You are the placebo: Making the mind matter*, Hay House UK, 2014

Eagleman, David. *Incognito: The Secret Lives of the Brain*, Canongate Canons, 2016

----------------------. *The Brain: The Story of You*, Canongate Books, 2016

Goggins, David. *Can't Hurt Me: Master Your Mind and Defy the Odds*, Lioncrest Publishing, 2018

Goldsmith, Marshall. Triggers: *What Got You Here Won't Get You There: How Successful People Become Even More Successful*, Profile Books, 2008

----------------------. *Creating Behavior That Lasts—Becoming the Person You Want to Be*, Penguin Random House USA, 2016

Hagemann, Hans W. *The Leading Brain: Neuroscience Hacks to Work Smarter, Better, Happier*, Tarcherperigee, 2018

Hofstede, Geert. *Cultures and Organizations: Software of the Mind*, McGraw-Hill Education, 2010

Isaac, Max and Belbin, Meredith. *Close the Interaction Gap*, Bridge Publishing, 2015

James Clear, *Atomic Habits: An Easy and Proven Way to Build Good Habits and Break Bad Ones*, Random House Business, 2018

Kahnman, Daniel. *Thinking, Fast and Slow*, Penguin, 2012

Lencioni, Patrick. *The Five Dysfunctions of a Team: A Leadership Fable,* John Wiley & Sons, 2002

----------------------. *The Advantage: Why Organizational Health Trumps Everything Else in Business*, John Wiley & Sons, 2012

Lewis, Richard. *When Cultures Collide: Leading Across Cultures*, Nicholas Brealey International, 2018

Mattone, John. *Intelligent Leadership: What You Need to Know to Unlock Your Full Potential*, AMACOM, 2013

----------------------. *Cultural Transformations: Lessons of Leadership and Corporate Reinvention,* John Wiley & Sons, 2016

----------------------. *The Intelligent Leader: Unlocking the 7 Secrets to Leading Others and Leaving Your Legacy,* John Wiley & Sons, 2019

McCarthy, Patti. *Cultural Chemistry: Simple Strategies for Bridging Cultural Gaps*, BookPOD, 2016

Mylett, Ed. *#MAXOUT YOUR LIFE,* Vervante, 2018

Olson, J. *Slight Edge*, Gazelle; 3rd edn, rev., 2013

Pink, Daniel H. *Drive: The Surprising Truth About What Motivates Us,* Canongate Books, 2018

Price, David Clive. *Age of Pluralism*, WildBlue Press, 2019

------------------------. Bamboo Strong, Wildblue Press 2019

Rapaille, Clotaire. *The Culture Code: An Ingenious Way to Understand Why People Around the World Buy and Live as They Do*, Broadway Books, 2007

Sharma, Robin. *The Leader Who Had No Title: A Modern Fable on Real Success in Business and in Life,* Simon & Schuster UK, 2010

Sinek, Simon. *Start With Why: How Great Leaders Inspire Everyone to Take Action*, Penguin, 2011

----------------------. *Leaders Eat Last: Why Some Teams Pull Together and Others Don't,* Penguin, 2017

Skinner, B.F. *Science And Human Behavior,* The Free Press; New Impression edition, 1965

Storr, Farrah. *The Discomfort Zone: How to Get What You Want by Living Fearlessly,* Piatkus, 2018

Thomas, D. A. and Ely, R. J. "Making Differences Matter: A New Paradigm for Managing Diversity," *Harvard Business Review,* 1996

Trompenaars, Fons. *Riding the Waves of Culture: Understanding Diversity in Global Business,* Nicholas Brealey Publishing, 2012

Acknowledgements

Uncommon Sense in Unusual Times is a distillation of 15 years of research into why people think and behave differently. Despite having a strong academic background, I am prouder of being a professional who has built businesses putting years of study into practice.

Along the way, I have had the privilege to work with leadership coaches and practitioners who make the best of the best even better and have also actively contributed to this book: Marshall Goldsmith, John Mattone, Dr Tony Alessandra, E.G. Sebastian and Dr David Clive Price.

My special thanks to the Global DISC master trainers who are equally passionate about empowering people to unlock their potential through the science of uncommon sense: Sinto Llobera, Anna Zelno, Wieke Gur, Janos Laincsek, and Gabor Holch.

The best part of my mission has been finding the right partners who share the same mindset and philosophy. They are the ICQpreneurs, the most active Global DISC licensees who all use the same tool but come from different backgrounds. This has the effect of making us complementary rather than competitive. ICQ Global would not exist without them. Thank you all.

The key lesson I learned when I set up my first company was that I was able to do anything but not everything. The only way to scale up a business is to be able to double down on your strengths and find the right partners who are able to see the vision and believe in it when others cannot. That is exactly what happened when I met Richard Sams (CEO of Mohara), who became my first partner with Robert Cubbage and Ben Blomerley. The next stage was made possible thanks to Skip Bowman (CEO of Global Mindset), who has also become part of this journey.

Last, but not least, my family. The iconic entrepreneurial great-grandfather I never met; my granny, who is a true inspiration in every way; and my mother, father, and brother, who have supported, or put up with me, even when I was not the most likeable member of the family. I suppose they did not really have much of an option, unlike Kasia, my fiancée. My life took a different turn when I met her, and she helped me realise some important 'life' lessons you can read about in the book. Kasia has gifted me with equal amounts of support, challenge to grow, and the chance to have fun, not to mention being part of the best decision of our lives, adopting Apocalypse and Destruction, our amazing felines.

About the Author

Csaba Toth is the founder of ICQ Global and the developer of the multi-award-winning Global DISC model.

Csaba has over 15 years of experience in setting up start-ups and working with entrepreneurs, coaches, and leaders of global businesses and Fortune 500 companies. His goal is to empower people to get along with themselves *and* others by understanding the blueprint of why people think and behave differently so they can turn those differences into synergy instead of painful liability.

Csaba has two master's degrees (his third, Executive MBA, is ongoing), and he is certified in leadership, intercultural, behavioural, psychometric, and organisational development frameworks.

His mission is to make the science of uncommon sense as uncomplicated and practical as possible, so people can actually apply it to unlock their own potential and bring out the best in others.

ICQ Global partners with companies to help them keep their best people and attract new talent by enabling management to lead in a way that makes employees and customers feel valued and understood.

The unique portfolio of data-driven assessments and training has already benefited organisations ranging from start-ups, to Fortune 500 companies, to national government agencies. It is also available through a global network of licensed practitioners.